PRAISES ~~FOR '14 WAYS TO~~
FIND YOUR AMAZING'

"The concept for finding your amazing is a must read that I'm certain will give readers 14 ways to problem-solve and find ways to cope with the challenges, setbacks, hurts and defeats that make you stagnant and rob you of the desire to go after your goals and dreams."
— **Chasity Melvin, former WNBA Basketball Player**

"Jennifer is one of the most purpose-driven people I know. It's amazing how she showed me how to utilize all my talents when it comes to giving back, thanks to her supreme leadership and dedication."
— **Antwan "Big Boi" Patton of the Iconic Rap Group OutKast**

"This is amazing! I am fully understanding of the reward in leaping into purpose!"
— **Satchel B. Jester, Scenes By Satchel, Contributing Editor at UPTOWN Magazine**

"Stagnating fear has been a constant hindrance in my life. Jennifer Lester has played a monumental role in helping me to find my purpose and use my why to overcome anxiety and tap into my ultimate purpose and potential."
— **Hazel Clark, 3-Time Olympian, Television Personality, Global sports and education ambassador**

"Jennifer's '14 ways to Find your Amazing' is more than a self-help book, it's a 'life guide' you will reference for years to come. It's not a book you'll lend to a friend but a book you'll want everyone in your life to have. Lester offers each of us a plan which is truly the way to find your amazing and live in your purpose; because purpose without a plan is simply passion. Manifest your authentic self and get your life guide with '14 Ways to Find Amazing'!"
— **Chrystale Wilson, Actress, Film Producer and Director**

"If you're looking for a book to help you finally break the mental chains that are holding you back, this is it. In her book, "14 Ways to Find Your Amazing," psychotherapist Jennifer Lester will guide you with actionable steps on a journey that will lead you to the life you've always imagined."
— **C. Denise Hendricks, Television Producer**

"Jennifer Lester is a true guru when it comes to matters of finding your purpose and connecting to your passions. She created an original and potent set of tools for cultivating your natural talent to live, take leaps of faith and enhancing your vision toward abundance. It will appeal to both those wanting timely advice and those seeking timeless wisdom and lifelong commitment. This books provides a path towards the process of developing your passions and takes a refreshing perspective towards passion, productivity and power."
— **Dr. Mathew Smith, Clinical Psychologist**

14 WAYS TO FIND YOUR *Amazing*

When Passion & Purpose Collide

JENNIFER SHEPHARD LESTER

ATLANTA, GEORGIA

14 Ways to Find Your Amazing: When Passion and Purpose Collide
Copyright © 2016 Jennifer Shephard Lester

Address inquiries to the publisher:

The Purpose Project
P.O. Box 831498
Stone Mountain, Georgia 30083

Learn more about the author at: www.thepurposeproject.com

ISBN: 978-0-9986694-1-0 (print)
ISBN: 978-0-9986694-0-3 (ebook)

Library of Congress Control Number: 2017902182

Printed in the United States of America

Edited by Annette R. Johnson, Allwrite Communications
Cover design and layout by Joey Shephard, QJS Design Studio

DEDICATION

My mom, Mary Ruth, my "reason"
My daughter, Temple, my "why" and
In memory of my dad, my "how"

My husband, Tommy, Thank You!

CONTENTS

INTRODUCTION

Purpose. It has perplexed many, inspired some and ruled others. Most religions and philosophies have some principle regarding it. People have searched the world over to recover their true purpose while others have yet to discover it. Some people seem to exude a sense of purpose while others appear to be sorely lacking it.

People are often stumped by the question: "What's your purpose?" How can you accurately answer something without really knowing what it is? Purpose is defined as the reason for which something exists or is done, made or used. It is doing what you love, as you dream and desire. It means living and leading a life of significance. It is your amazing, or what makes you special, interesting and appealing. It makes you smile and gives you a sense of fulfillment.

When I started on a journey to find my amazing, I began to gather facts, collect notes, and identify patterns in individuals who were living their purpose. They were undeniably living with **passion, productivity** and **power**. When your daily work lights your fire, that's passion. That which fills us with passion, motivates our productivity. When we are passionate and productive with respect to a career, an endeavor, or cause, it is the source of great power.

Everyone has a purpose; however, not everyone has found it. I created the Purpose Project to help others get connected with their purpose, enhance their vision to see beyond perceived limitations, and generally make their lives fuller and richer. For years, I have read books such as the *Celestine Prophecy* while studying the law of attraction, following the teachings of Napoleon Hill, and gaining inspiration from Oprah Winfrey. In all my studies, there is one common theme, one common thread: "You." Your life depends on you – your thoughts, your actions, all of it! Throughout my years in counseling clients, I've concluded that nothing will work unless you do.

I am also sure of these life principles: it doesn't matter your size but the magnitude of your heart; neither your location but your destination; nor your speed but your direction. In the end, it's how you look at life. Your perception of yourself and the world will shape your reality. If you have the courage or bravery to follow your heart and live intentionally, you can change the world by changing the one person who matters most – you. When purpose and passion collide, amazing things begin to happen.

Confucius once said, "Choose a job you love, and you never have to work a day in your life." That said, if money weren't an issue, what would you do? What kind of hobby, career or cause would you engage in? Although money isn't everything, it's right up there with oxygen. You need it to survive. You were born to do more than just go to work, pay bills and die. The key is to find your passion, for it will lead to your purpose. It is much easier to get motivated about something that you are excited about than to get motivated about something that does not interest you. Find a way to do what you love even if you have to do what you must until you can do what we want. When you are able to do what you love, it fuels further dreams and desires. That is part of what purpose is all about.

The world doesn't revolve around me, but it certainly knows I'm here. I learned very early in life that I had magic. I was able to talk, and people would listen. Not only would they listen, but they believed my words. I felt a deep connection with people – even total strangers. People I would've just met would start telling me their life story. I grew up in the era when children should be "seen and not heard," but I talked a lot at school, home, and anywhere. My dad would constantly say, "Child, you talk too much. I hope you make some money from running your mouth."

Even as a child, I was aware of how my words could bring people to tears or make them laugh. I remember once being angry at my brother and screaming, "I wish you weren't my brother, and I don't want to live here!"

My father looked at me and sternly said, "Watch your mouth. There is life and death in your tongue." I wasn't totally sure what my dad meant at the time, but I knew it felt serious. From that point forward, I learned to "watch my mouth."

Even though we all chanted the children's rhyme "sticks and stones may break my bones, but words can never hurt me," at some point in our lives we realized that was completely untrue. Words can and do hurt. Words can influence us, inspire us or just as easily bring us to tears. Words have a powerful and undeniably overwhelming influence on us – for good and, at times, for bad.

Today, as a professional, licensed therapist, I listen empathi-cally with unconditional positive regard, providing words of hope and wisdom combined with a splash of humor. This allows me to be heard and believable. People must believe the messenger before they believe the message. Words change our relationships, our demeanor, and our entire system of beliefs. Words, my friends, can change everything! Words have a dramatic effect on what we know, how we interact with people and the decisions we ultimately make.

One day while I was speaking at an event, I started talking about "magic." I explained that we all have magic and that every great magician has a

> *"Purpose and laughter are the twins that must not be separated. Each is empty without the other."*
>
> –Robert K. Greenleaf

magic word to release his power. In fact, the word "abracadabra" is Hebrew for "I create what I speak." Words have power; they give us our magic. I followed that by talking about two of the most important words: "I am." What follows them will shape your future and ultimately change your life. After my speech, a lady came up and began to share her story with me. She said, "Your throat chakra is open, and your voice will land on the ears of many." I immediately thought of what my dad had always said to me, "There is life and death in your tongue."

I was unfamiliar with chakras, but I knew it had something to do with Hindu. I researched it and learned that the throat chakra is the fifth chakra, and it is the first of the higher or spiritual chakras on the "chakra ladder." This chakra is located in the region of neck and shoulders, and its color is blue. The gift of this chakra is accepting your originality, expressing your authentic voice and speaking your truth. As I continued to research the throat chakra, I learned that the energy of this chakra allows you to seek knowledge that is true, beyond limitations of time and space, and beyond cultural and family conditioning. The main challenge for the fifth chakra is doubt and negative thinking. When you gain and verify your knowledge through meditation and direct experience, then doubt and negativity are removed. It is the way of standing up for what you believe, saying no when you need to, and being open and honest. The fifth chakra is linked directly to your integrity and a sense of honor. As a communication center, it not only allows you to express who you are and what you stand for, but also allows you to listen deeply to another. A person with an open throat chakra is a good listener, enabling another person to have the experience of being heard, one of the most profound human needs. All of that described me. In fact, this is what I do as a career and is my life's calling. I help people accept their truth, tell their story in an inspiring way and find their amazing. Likewise, this book intends to help readers find their amazing, which is synonymous with finding one's purpose.

In helping readers find their amazing, the book is organized into four major themes, which are relegated as chapters. Each theme, builds on the other, such that the readers not only find their amazing, but they will likely inspire or help others to do the same. You're not on the path to simply finding a new job or career; you are moving toward living on purpose, not dictated by life's demands. You see, a career is what you're paid for, but a calling is what you're made for.

Up to my last days, I want to live very intentionally and deliberately, full of passion and purpose. I don't want to leave here owing this world anything. In my last breath, I want to be able to say that I have done everything that I had in my heart. My hope is that you would, too. On this life's journey, if you are brave enough to start on the path to find your amazing, life-changing things can happen for you, as well as those around you.

The benefit of finding your passion goes beyond self-fulfillment. Leading a purposeful life inspires and motivates others. When others see your light shining, they'll be inspired to shine theirs, too. I uncovered my purpose by being willing to be uncomfortable and fearless, not knowing whether I would succeed or fail. Ultimately, I have succeeded enough to be fulfilled and now inspire others – like you.

The book is divided into four basic units, which comprise the Amazing Model (pictured). Each unit overlaps in significance and interdependence. Within each unit are fuller expressions of its meaning and actualization that, in totality, encompass the 14 ways to find your amazing. Thus, in general, you should come to espouse vision, preparation, faith, and gratitude in the journey to amazing.

UNIT 1
HONORING YOUR CALLING

Preparation

Vision   Amazing   Faith

Gratitude

Suppose you just jumped in a random car and started driving without any sense of your destination or even information about the car itself. People would call you "misguided," among many other choice names. Similarly, some people's lives are just like this. They have no idea where they are headed, but they feel somewhat satisfied that they are at least moving in a direction. That's no way to live, being alive but lost – without a clear objective or any idea why and how to get one.

The car represents you; the fuel represents your purpose; the road represents life's paths; and the destination represents fulfillment. If you know nothing about the car (you), how will you know what type of fuel to use or maintenance it requires? If you don't know what road (path) to take, how will you arrive at your destination (fulfillment)? If you have no fuel (purpose) or the wrong kind, how can you begin or continue on your journey?

Nothing makes us feel more alive and brings us greater joy than pursuing a calling that is aligned with our passion and gifts. In fact, a clear vision of our life's purpose is crucial to our sense of fulfillment. Like the car in the example, we must first be willing to examine ourselves, understanding our distinctive abilities, divine gifts, strengths, interests, and life experiences. To realize our destination, we must recognize where we came from, where we are now, and where we are going. We will only know where we are going when we know who we really are. We can only get to where we are supposed to go when we have enough conviction or passion about getting there. Our life purpose keeps us going, and when one goal is met, it redirects us to another. Thus, we are never lost and aimlessly searching.

Our life's purpose is something fulfilling to which we can easily devote our entire lives. We refer to this as a "calling" because it is divinely inspired but naturally fulfilled. Therefore, while our purpose is something that feels right, it is also something we can ignore or overlook. When we honor it, we feel whole and happy, but when we ignore it, we feel frustrated and dissatisfied. Oprah Winfrey once said, "When you're honoring your calling, there's an undeniable sense of stimulation and exhilaration. It just feels so right."

> *"Honor your calling; everyone has one. Trust your heart and success will come to you."*
>
> – Oprah Winfrey

I began to notice that anything in life that was in line with my purpose felt good and was enjoyable. I also recognized that anything that went against my purpose felt bad and was uncomfortable. When you get an understanding of why you are here and what your purpose is, it allows you to see a clear path of where you should go. Having a purpose gives you the courage, determination and insight to find your direction. Otherwise, you are just wandering. You become a nomad, and you may spend a lifetime never reaching a purpose-filled destination.

In the Walt Disney animated film "Tinker Bell," the writer did an excellent job of demonstrating how not honoring our calling can be a disaster. Although this movie is intended for children, many adults could learn a few things about honoring their calling. In the film, each new fairy learns her talent. In fact, their talent picks them. In Pixie Hollow, the place where the fairies live, Tinker Bell becomes friends with other fairies who have different talents. A Water Fairy, Garden Fairy, Animal Fairy, and a Light Fairly are among her new friends. Tinker Bell learns that her talent is to be one of the tinkers, the fairies who make and fix things. Prior to this revelation, Tinker Bell compared her talent to the others. She tried to learn their craft, thinking what they do is more glamorous. She tried her hand at making dewdrops, lighting fireflies, and trying to teach baby birds to fly. However, she failed miserably at all of these. One day on the beach, Tinker Bell found parts of a music box and figured out how to put them together to repair the box. When the other fairy friends witnessed her doing this, they told her that she was tinkering and that she should be proud of her talent. In the end, Tinker Bell used her natural ability to help the fairies save Spring.

Much like Tinker Bell, when we try our hand at talents that are not our given talents, we can expect that things won't go smoothly or we will feel unhappy. We are out of alignment, dishonoring our innate gifting. Although each one of us has a different purpose, many of us will not fulfill, or honor, that calling because of personal, familial or societal encoding. In other words, we get our programming, or mindset, from a singular or collective influence. For instance, if your parents have always told you that you can't do something, then you will probably never attempt it. If society mainly dictates that your interests should only be undertaken by people unlike you, then you probably may never attempt it. Many of the barriers to manifesting our life's purpose come from cultural thoughtforms, a lack of exposure, and other people, particularly those close to you. Furthermore, in a close personal relationship, people tend to take on the goals and the thoughtforms of others. So how do we overcome adverse encoding, which misdirects us from our purpose? In the next sections, you will learn more about the main aspects to honoring your calling that can redirect you toward finding your amazing, your life's purpose.

1.

WHY YOU WERE CREATED

A sking someone, "Why was I created?" is almost like asking that person to be God or you. No one can define your life's purpose for you. It is a vision that either lay dormant or active within you, which first begins in deciding that YOU MATTER. You are unique and different from everyone else, meaning you are special. Your purpose works in tandem with your values and interests. Combined, they give you the unwavering belief in what you stand for and ensures you live based on divine design, not someone else's making.

You were created to do your part, or play your role in this life. This means that you must first believe with every fiber of your being that there is a purpose, or reason, for your life. Famed self-help author Napoleon Hill stated, "There is one quality that one must possess to win, and that is definiteness of purpose, the knowledge of what one wants and the burning desire to possess it." According to Hill, in order to win in life, you must have a clear purpose. Hill goes on to say, "There is no hope of success for the person who does not have a central purpose, or definite goal at which to aim."

Many people struggle with finding the answer and just simply making life choices. Why am I here? What is the purpose of my life? The stress and anxiety in trying to figure this out often adds more pressure. The answer to your question has always existed. When we realize that it's more about truly believing there is an answer, we will relax and allow the awareness to come to us rather than chasing it. You will then have a shift that is aligned with the universal flow, which means you should forget about needing to make a choice. Your higher consciousness has already chosen. Instead of searching for answers, look first for the blockages you can expose and release. Then you can look for the gift of "beingness" that is wanting to come through you. Look for it to come, feel it, embrace it, attune to it, give it wings, and let it flow freely through you. The answers in which you seek will then happen naturally. In that moment, you'll truly change not only yourself, but also the world around you.

There has always been an emphasis on outward productivity – doing rather than being – in our culture. Thus, rather than focusing on inner peace, joy, love, and compassion, we focus on accomplishments. For many, a sense of limited time directs our decision-making. We feel we must accomplish this or that by a certain age or be considered a failure. We confound that further with a sense that everything must be done a certain way. The truth is that you have all the time you need to accomplish things that are part of your life's

> *"Success is not to be pursued. It is to be attracted by the person you become."*
>
> – Jim Rohn

purpose, and your means to accomplish this may be very different than it is for others. Still, you can rest assured that you have all the resources you need to accomplish your purpose.

If you do not feel you have enough time to accomplish what you are currently undertaking, then I will say that what you are doing is probably not your purpose. When you are embarking on your life's purpose, you will have enough time or you will create the time. You will find it so joyful that everything else falls away, and determination, focus, and concentration will emerge. If there is anything you are forcing yourself to do out of duty or obligation (guilt), or out of feeling that people will admire or respect you when you do it (affirmation), then you are probably not honoring the light of your soul.

Sometimes we make things harder than they need to be. If you stop complicating your life's purpose, you will clearly see it. Stop trying to force it. Stop trying to figure it out, and instead use our highest expression, love, in these moments of anxiety. The universe will use its unlimited power to support the gift of love and acceptance we express to ourselves. Therefore, we don't need to figure out why we are here or what we need to do. We just need to be willing and open to accept what the universe reveals to us.

Journey to Amazing

As you consider your life's purpose, ask yourself: What would I do if I were alone? If no one else in my life would gain or lose from what I do, would it change my choices? What would I do for myself? What would bring me peace and joy? What if society did not exist or had absolutely different values, would I still like what I am doing?

Sometimes you're just not the best judge of what makes you happy. Ask the people who know you intimately when you seem the happiest and what you do the most enthusiastically. Their answers may surprise you.

2.

VISION IS WHEN YOU SEE IT

Some people spend a lifetime searching for their purpose. They are wandering souls on a mission to find it. Oftentimes, the thing that we search for is right under our nose, right in front of our face. Blinded by our own expectations, we often miss it. As we seek to find our purpose, we must understand that it was never lost or hidden. It is we ourselves who have lost sight of the very reason we exist. When we remove the blinders and adjust our focus, we can begin to have a clearer view. We then move from just having sight to having vision.

There are many synonyms for "vision." Dream, revelation, prophecy, and goal are a few that come to mind. A vision is a lingering image or an idea that you have in mind for yourself, your career, your family or any other future endeavor. Clarity of that vision helps you to pursue passions, accomplish goals and produce a more successful, favorable outcome in general. A clear vision will open the mind to endless possibilities and unlimited opportunities. Having a vision is one of the most important factors in the path to a purposeful life, for you must first see it and then believe it in order to achieve it.[1]

Don't confuse sight and vision, however. Human beings begin to develop sight during the fourth week of pregnancy. Cells from the developing brain tissue begin to come together to start forming two optic nerves, one on each side of the head. Around the same time, cells found on an outer layer of the fetus begin developing into what will eventually become the lens of the eye, which will help your baby focus his eyes on objects both near and far. Although sight is developed early in life, vision comes much later for many of us.

Having a vision for your life is an important key to success. It establishes whether you win or lose, and more importantly, how you define what is a victory or loss. It drives how, when, where, and what you receive and possess. By having a vision and achieving goals related to it, people feel valuable, exposing the potential they have inside them.

> *"Your vision will become clear only when you can look into your own heart. Who looks outside, dreams; who looks inside, awakes."*
>
> ~ Carl Jung

Throughout my years training and coaching, when I ask people to list qualities of a good leader, one of the first things that they name is a "visionary." This, in fact, is one of the tenet qualities needed to be a leader. Vision is the ability to see beyond your current reality, mentally creating and inventing what does not now exist in order to become what you know can be. A vision is important in all aspects of life: personally, professionally, and corporately. When you have a vision, you can overcome obstacles and persevere through tough times because you having a knowing. A well-defined vision helps you to focus on goals that achieve your purpose. Its attainment becomes your measurement for your success. If you do not have a vision of who you want to be, how you want to succeed or what you want out of life, you begin to lack drive, and your life becomes just a random string of events. A clear vision connects your passions and greatest potential. Regardless of what is going on in the world or challenges that present themselves, having a vision clarifies what you do and why you are doing them.

Vision can be used in two different ways: inspiration and prediction. It is used to inspire you to attain something that you desire. Without vision, you focus on surviving rather than thriving. A vision is one of the most powerful ways to keep you focused on what you want to achieve in life while keeping you motivated in accomplishing it. It is also used in the prediction of potential changes and opportunities. In this way, we remain optimistic because we anticipate a better future. A vision will open up your mind to many new possibilities for a more promising future. When you can envision a future that is happier, healthier, and more productive, you are more likely to make the changes that are necessary for you to reach the life you want.[2]

The expression of your vision should be emotional, physical, spiritual, and intellectual. Thus, the process of connecting with your vision is intricate. You must see with your mind and soul, not with your physical eyes. There are moments in which things you see with your physical eyes contradict the vision for your life. This is why our vision should be aligned with our passions and purpose. Otherwise, we may lose faith, second-guessing or abandoning our vision. To avoid this, make a mental picture of what you desire based on your values and interests. Then add complementary feelings and emotions to that mental picture. Imagine you giving every effort for its completion. Then give thanks like you've received it already while keeping your emotions parallel to the vision. In doing this, you are giving positive energy to that desire, so your vision will come to fruition and manifest into something beyond your wildest dreams.

In James Allen's book *As a Man Thinketh,* he writes, "All that a man achieves and all that he fails to achieve is the direct result of his own thoughts." Your thoughts and your vision are connected, and sometimes they are one in the same. Since all material things move from non-physical to physical reality, our vision and its goals are paramount in the process of achievement. Our vision and focus act like a magnet that attracts and connects the pieces together. When we focus our brain on what we want, we actually increase the amplitude of the cellular vibration of our mind, body and soul.

> *"Everything in life is vibration."*
>
> – Albert Einstein

The "law of vibration" states everything is energy in its most basic form and, thus, yields a vibration (electromagnetic frequency) and movement. One summer, my daughter went to science camp. She came home excited to ask me a riddle she had learned. She asked, "Why can't you trust an atom? Because it makes up everything," she exclaimed. She learned a brief lesson on chemistry. The joke was funny yet true. Everything is comprised of atoms. Atoms are in a constant state of motion, and depending on the speed of these atoms, things appear as a solid, liquid or gas. Therefore, if everything is made up of atoms, that also includes us. Humans are made of cells, which are made of atoms. These atoms are comprised of subatomic particles, and the particles are actually just vibrating energy, always in motion. We all know that sound is a vibration, but so are thoughts and feelings. Everything that manifests itself in your life is there because it matches the vibration from your thoughts. Thus, we can be strongly impacted – either positively or negatively – by vibrational energy or frequency. In essence, I always say, "A person is limited only by the thoughts that he or she chooses." Thus, we must choose thoughts that yield positive energy that can propel us to the fulfillment of our vision.

Journey to Amazing

Creating a compelling vision for your life is one of the most effective tactics for achieving your dreams. The best way to look at the life-vision concept is like a GPS that helps guide you to take the best course of actions. This will set you on a path that will help propel you toward your amazing life. A well-defined vision won't happen overnight. It will require time and reflection. Consider every aspect of your life: personal and professional, tangible and intangible.

Your life's vision should not be confused with your long-term goals. Goals are individual accomplishments you strive toward. Your life's vision defines who you are and what you want to be known for. Your vision helps define the goals.

Write down the vision you have for your life. It should consist of an overall description of your ideal life. When you begin the process of creating a vision for your life, start by identifying your purpose. If you're not sure what your purpose is, consider your passions and core values. Make sure you're not too generic. Your vision should exemplify your values and your view of the future, so be clear and very specific.

Keep in mind, your vision may also change over time. The point is to have one so you know why you're doing what you do and you're more fulfilled doing it. Remember that a life of fulfillment does not usually happen by chance, but by design.

3.

TRUSTING YOUR INSTINCTS

You can't expect anyone to understand your vision because it wasn't given to them. That means you'll have to trust your instincts, what you sense as being supernaturally or divinely imparted to you. Carl Jung says, "Your vision will become clear only when you look in your heart. Who looks outside, dreams; who looks inside, awakes." There is a little voice inside each of us. This voice is our guide to a life of greatness. Power, ingenuity, and genius emerge from your heart and mind when you let your inner voice guide your life. Your inner voice puts you on track to live on purpose.

Your inner voice is one voice competing with a thousand outer voices. They others appear to be louder, stronger and wiser, but it's only a perception. The voices of our parents, friends, media and society often drown our inner voice. Our little voice is that guiding light that, if followed, will move us to the next level. It will help us find our way and put us one step closer to our purpose, goals and dreams. Oftentimes, we are afraid, so we doubt ourselves or we let someone else's voice guide our light.

A bird sitting on a tree is not afraid of the branch breaking because its trust is not in the branch but in her own wings. This is much like trusting your instincts. You can only truly trust your wings if you truly believe in yourself. I challenge you to find any extremely successful person who doesn't greatly believe in themselves. These successful people are basically no different than you and I, as we are all endowed with talent, opportunities and various resources. The only difference is their astounding belief in themselves. They are able to persevere and achieve success because of their level of belief in themselves despite the number of failures that they have experienced.

Essentially, the bird sitting on the branch has "self-trust," which means that she trusts herself enough to take care of her needs and her safety, as well as trusting herself to survive situations. It also means that she refuses to give up or second-guess herself. The reason you may not trust yourself is because of fear and limiting beliefs that appear in the form of negative self-talk, which is a major factor that holds us back from following our instincts. When we learn to talk to ourselves like champions rather than listen to ourselves as victims, we build our self-trust. Second-guessing your instincts causes all those around you to second-guess your decisions, choices, and advice. When you're not sure, it shows up in all aspects of your life. Surely, you can't expect anyone to believe in you if you don't believe in yourself.

Many of us have experienced that unexplainable sense of knowing something, sometimes called a "hunch" or intuition. For instance, you may intuitively decide to take a different route to work and later learn that you missed a 20-car pileup on the highway.

Maybe something just told you to play the lottery and you won.

A lady in New York recalled having an unyielding urge to leave her desk and walk down the street to get coffee. This was odd because she would never leave the building except on rare occasions for lunch or to go home. Well, that particular day, she followed her instinct to leave, and moments later, as she walked to get coffee on September 11, 2001, her building was hit by an aircraft. What if she had used logic instead of her intuition? Logically, she had no real reason to leave the building, especially as this was not her routine. Her intuition, though, saved her life. Like second-guessing, intellect can often be the enemy of intuition.

Intuition's enemy, intellect, causes you to overthink or second-guess so you miss critical intuitive cues, such as a little funny tingle and strange urge. These gut feelings are sometimes called your innate wisdom. Researchers continue to try to "logically" explain this innate wisdom. According to many researchers, intuition is far more material than it seems. Social psychologist Dr. David Myers explained that the intuitive right brain is almost always "reading" our surroundings, even when our conscious left brain is otherwise engaged. The subconscious can register this information while the conscious mind remains blissfully unaware of what's going on.[3]

> *"Be willing to trust your instincts, especially if you cannot find answers elsewhere."*
>
> – Brian Koslow

It's hard to trust your instinct when you are not sure what your instincts are trying to tell you. This takes us back to "trust." Some people know themselves better than others and thus have more experience in trusting their instincts. Developing a trust in your instincts requires practice, which means allowing yourself to make mistakes so you can learn from them. In order for you understand how critical your intuition or instincts are to your life, try not trusting them in any given situation. Usually, you will end up saying, "Something told me not to do that" or "I had feeling that wasn't right."

Sometimes the issue is knowing when it's truly your gut instinct or whether it's an indulgent impulse. Like the woman in the September 11th example, your instincts require faith or trust, but impulses don't. When we learn to identify which signals to focus on – whether they're clammy palms, a funny feeling in your stomach, or a mysterious feeling that something is up – we move toward or down the path to finding our amazing. Honestly, you'll be lost on this journey and never arrive on your life's intended destination without your innate compass, your intuition.

Like animals, humans have instincts, genetically hard-wired behaviors that enhance our ability to cope with vital environmental contingencies. Trusting your gut is so powerful because your gut has been cataloging tons information all of your life. That invaluable catalog is a collection of all your subconscious experiences and observations. The human brain's catalog also includes intellectual thoughts and descriptive words to make sense of our environment and the world as a whole. This catalog influences our actions and feelings whether we realize it or not.

Logic is designed to take you from A to Z, but imagination, intuition and instinct will take you to where you're purposefully meant to be. However, you can't completely dismiss logic, so you have to recognize when your gut feelings should supplant, accompany or abandon logic. Once you notice the intuitive signals, you must activate your mind to shift through your choices and take the best action. Remember to "follow your heart, but take your mind with you."

I met an ER doctor who was interested in life coaching. She was unhappy in her career and wanted to change her life. In our brief conversation, she stated she didn't want to be a doctor anymore. I simply replied, "You never wanted to be a doctor anyway." What she wanted was to gain admiration, respect and external praise. She wanted to please her family, make momma proud, and of course, the money was pretty good. When we give up who we are to please others, what we really give up is internal peace and the opportunity to make a viable contribution in this world. When you live for the applause of other people, you will also live in fear of their disapproval. Often, our truest passions emerge in childhood, only to be squashed by real-life pressures. Think about what you loved long before you had to worry about working or supporting others. Did you enjoy baking, running, writing, painting or doing class experiments? Getting back in touch with those inclinations is an important step in finding your passion and purpose.

You are happier and fulfilled when doing what's most important to you and expressing it in every aspect of your life. To find out what matters most to you and ultimately define your purpose, it requires delving into your life from various angles to discover any matching themes. In doing so, listen to your intuition, the little voice inside you. What does it immediately say to you? Ask yourself: What do I love doing in my spare time or when working? What activities do I currently do that I enjoy or would do for free? What do I naturally do well?

There is no better way of creating a more fulfilling life than by mastering the art of tuning into your most inspired and ingenious self, your inner voice. As your voice on the inside grows in clarity and strength, so will your inspiration when you listen. The universe is the ultimate "radio," and we each vibrate at our own frequency. When you begin to attune to that inspiring station from within, it will guide you to new levels of creativity and operation. Your wisdom and fulfillment are expanded through such careful listening. Communing with this wise inner guide will help you create a greater contribution to others and possibly even a legacy. Many great spiritual revelations and mental attributes are suddenly birthed from within you when your voice on the inside becomes louder than the many outside voices or opinions.

You cannot attune to this inspiring voice without living a more inspiring life. The secret of tuning into its magnificent messages is having a heart filled with love, which means having joy and gratitude toward all things. When your heart is open wide with love, your inner voice becomes loud and clear, and your most life-expanding messages enter into your mind with ease. If your heart is filled with love, it is almost impossible to stop your inner voice from speaking clearly and profoundly.

Journey to Amazing

The little nudges from your soul, inspirational thoughts and unexplainable feeling or image in your mind are all a part of your inner wisdom. There is nothing more important than being attuned to your inner voice. Your inner voice not only knows your deepest thoughts, but it is your deepest thoughts. This is a much-needed power that must be mastered to truly live the life you were meant to have! Most of the time, your inner voice is in conflict with outward motives. You concern yourself with what society thinks or what your parents, friends, or love ones might think. Often those who love you the most can be the ones who most hold you back — not through their negativity, but through their idea of love. This could be their wanting what they think is best for you, their wanting you to be there for them, or their desire for you to live up to their vision and goals for your life. As you look at your life's purpose, look at who you are close to in your life, and ask: Have you been manifesting what they wanted for you? Are you clear about what you want for yourself?

Learn to quiet the voices that are not your own. To master this, you must learn what your inner voice sounds like in a crowd. Oftentimes, your elevation will require isolation. If you have trouble identifying your inner voice from the others, silence all of them, and then quiet your mind totally. This will take practice, meditation, and spending time with yourself and your thoughts. Once you've done that, focus only on your gut-feelings. When you listen to others' voices, identify which remarks are consistent with your gut-feelings. Now follow that, and let it lead you to a purposeful life.

4.

FOLLOWING YOUR PASSION

Doing things that you are passionate about takes little effort. It comes natural, so you do them with ease. You get lost in time; you fall in love. The feeling you get from doing what you love is much like a relationship. Think about your first love, that special someone who you couldn't stop thinking about. In love, you forget to eat and can hardly sleep. It makes you smile and gives you tingles or even butterflies. Yes, it's love. Similarly, that's the feeling that your life's work should give you. It should give you a feeling of euphoria and send you in a place where there is

> *"You can only become truly accomplished at something you love. Don't make money your goal. Instead pursue the things you love doing and then do them so well that people can't take their eyes off of you."*
>
> – Maya Angelou

neither space nor time. Best-selling author Christopher Howard says that you should "allow your business and your life to be an expression of your soul's purpose."

Just like a relationship, your pursuits require nourishment or they will wither like a once beautiful flower. It is not just enough to love something or someone. You have to invest in the relationship to make it work, giving your time, energy and resources along with compromising, negotiating, and having patience.

On a trip to Charleston, South Carolina, I took a tour of a famous plantation. I learned that Charleston was at the center of the slave trade in America. It was a very enlightening, informative and rather spiritual tour. To actually see slave quarters and relive accounts of their lives on the plantation stirred some emotions. It also sparked this question: Are you a master or a slave of life? If you are unsure of the answer, ask yourself: "Why do I do this?" This will reveal whether you are a master or a slave of life. If the answer is "because I have no choice," then you are a slave. A master's answer will be "because I choose to do it." A slave feels that he is forced to do something. Therefore, he has no power to choose and is a victim of circumstances. Outside voices have become his master. When these external voices or influences are so loud that they dictate how a person dresses, the career he chooses, and even his self-image, then that person is in captivity.

On the other hand, a master feels that he is doing something out of choice; therefore, he has freedom to choose and is empowered to do so. He hears the voice of others and is quite aware that they exist. However, he chooses his own voice to guide his life. The difference in feeling between the two has nothing to do with the actual happening. Both the master and the slave may be doing the exact same thing under the same circumstance, but one feels empowered while the other feels powerless. The rationale behind this is that the master chooses his own path while the slave follows someone else's. As we seek mastery, pay attention to what is pushing you and what is pulling you. There is a difference, and depending on which one compels you, that will determine the amount of control you have over your own life's journey. When you're being pulled or magnetized, life is leading you in the direction of your passions. You are being attracted to your soul's desire. On the other hand, when you are being pushed, it is usually on a path that may not be aligned with your gifts or passion. The more clearly focused we are on exactly what we want and know to be our true calling, the easier and faster we'll manifest everything we need to make it a physical reality.

Your calling is exactly that. It is what you are called to do, but the calling itself is not everything, meaning what's next? When someone calls you on the phone or in person, you don't simply answer by acknowledging the call. You respond with further dialogue or action. In other words, there is no period at the end of the sentence; it is more like a semicolon. Likewise, you have to recognize and then activate your calling. What I've found is that the universe doesn't reward half-hearted pleas.

There is a simple formula to figuring out your purpose. It is that thing that you love to do that you'll do for free, but you do it so well that others will pay you for it. Pretty simple! Are you currently pursuing or operating in your passion? Or are you like the many people who are in pursuit of wealth, fame, fortune and social acceptance? Meanwhile, it is the people with passion that will change the world. Talent isn't much without passion.

If you don't know your purpose, follow your passion. That will lead you to your purpose. I often tell people that I've been a counselor and life-coach since 4th grade. When I decided to leave my job after 14 years, it was simply to pursue what I love. I knew with every fiber of my being it was the right thing. I knew it because while work was somewhat fulfilling, I wasn't in love with it and it still felt like work. I knew my calling was in therapy and counseling. I found ways to do it even when no one asked me to, even if it was unpaid, unsolicited and unappreciated. I did it because it made me feel alive. I simply loved it.

> *"There is no passion to be found settling for the life that you are cable of living."*
>
> – Nelson Mandela

When you're not sure what you love or what you're passionate about, remember what you loved as a child. Our truest passion emerges in childhood. Think about what you loved long before you worried about a career. If money weren't a factor what would you do? When financial pressures dictate your choices in career you rarely end up doing what you're most passionate about. If you trust the process, your career will ultimately lead to financial security. When your purpose and passion collide, magical things happen. People are unable to take their eyes off you, and that, my friend, is where the value lies.

There will be many people who do what you do, but no one will do it like you do. Whenever you're engaged in the business of who you're meant to be, you will be more awake, alive and active, ready to play a vital part in the world. Although your work may be similar to someone else's, when you're operating in your calling, no one has your magic. No one's cakes will taste just like yours. No one will deliver a speech like you. No one will be able to strategically plan like you. Don't worry about who has already done it. You just do it better or differently. People don't buy what you do; they buy how you do.

Journey to Amazing

The best way to unearth your passions is to follow these steps. Start with getting back in touch with those instincts you had as a child. Most of us know exactly who we are and what would make us happiest. If money were no object, what would you do? Of course, money can't be ignored, but don't let financial pressures dictate all your choices. When you are working your magic (what you're passionate about) it should ultimately lead to financial security, but if financial security is the defining motivator, it's unlikely you'll end up doing what you love. Do what you love and love what you do. Next, take an inventory of your talents. Focus on the things that you both enjoy and do well, and write them down. Then narrow the list to the top three or four things you would do even without payment. Now notice when you lose track of time. What would you love to spend hours doing that you never have enough time to do or that you long to do more of? That is a passion. Review your lists and keep them handy, using them as your starting point to finding your amazing vision of the future.

UNIT 2
SHARPENING YOUR SKILLS

Things don't just happen by chance or happenstance. It doesn't matter if you're in a relatively simple weight loss program or supportive multi-level marketing group, your results or success depends on your determination. All these self-betterment programs can work but not unless you are committed, dedicated and inspired, singularly devoted to seeing a task through to the end. We've all heard the phrase, "Good things come to those who wait," but may I add this: "but only what's left behind by those who hustle."

Don't get caught up in the get-rich-quick mentality. This kind of microwave success is unrealistic. For the most part, we see the rewards of the most successful people's journey, but we rarely see the behind-the-scenes sacrifices, including sleep, relationships, and lifestyle. Eddie Conner, a comedian, actor and founder of the March of Dimes, said, "It took me 20 years to become an overnight success. The only time success comes before work is in the dictionary. The difference between who you are and who you want to be is simply discipline."

Over the years, I've realized that self-discipline is rooted in every measure of success. It's an invisible super-power that you may not be able to smell or taste, but it has massive impact on outcomes. Discipline can transform fat into fit, depression into happiness, uneducated into an expert, and poor into rich. We can either generate great excuses or great results. It's like darkness and light; the existence of light eliminates darkness. Once self-discipline is injected into any negative situation, the outcome begins to brighten.

Although we tell ourselves that we want success and positive results, our actions aren't always consistent with that desire. Our words express who we want to be, but our actions express who we really are. So, in the end, the old expression "action speaks louder than words" holds true in our quest to turn passion into purpose. Much like your life's purpose, or your calling, you must be willing to do what it takes to make it emerge in excellence, which means being dedicated to sharpening your craft. People who are the best at anything, those we call "amazing," typically adhere to a rigorous, consistent training and practice regimen. In other words, they are dedicated to sharpening their skill.

5.

HARD WORK BEATS TALENT

Perhaps you think that success is only available to those who are naturally gifted or who are "born lucky." Maybe you've made a few conclusions about their success, including statements such as: "They just got lucky," "They were in the right place at the right time," "They were just born into the right family," or "Favor ain't fair." In some cases, these statements can be true, but for the most part, a person's success is the result of preparation and hard work. In response to all of those quotes about luck and divine favor, one could respond, saying, "Anything worth having, you have to work hard for it," "Faith without works is dead," or "Nothing makes success more likely than preparation." The Roman philosopher Seneca said it best: "Luck is what happens when preparation meets opportunity."

We all have endowed talents, which simply means a natural tendency to be good at a particular thing. A talent can vary from person to person, but it generally means your natural ability to do something well or better than most other people. Talent can be developed and expanded through hard work, but it's usually a natural sort of gifting for a particular thing. People who are said to be 'talented' are those who have achieved greatness in their particular area of interest. People like, for example, Whitney Houston was named by *Rolling Stone* as one of the top vocalist in the world. While the late Grammy Award-winning singer obviously had a natural ability, she also had a pernicious substance abuse habit that eventually diminished her signing ability and was responsible for her early demise. Thus, talent can get you there, but it can't keep you there. Only character can do that.

Have you ever wondered why some of the most talented people are some of the least successful people? Talent isn't the whole story. While it plays a significant role in one's success, there are certain character traits that must accompany it. Talent is the fuel for the fire. It will kick start you toward success and make things easier to get going in the beginning. However, if you have someone who is very talented but doesn't work hard and someone who is not talented but works really hard, the person who works hard is usually going to succeed to a greater extent. In fact, the talented person who doesn't work hard, may not succeed at all.

We have all heard the classic tale of the "Tortoise and the Hare." The boastful hare brags about how he's never been beaten in a race, but the persistent tortoise accepts the challenge and wins. The moral of the story is "slow and steady wins the race." However, I often challenge this popular

> *"The only place success comes before work is in the dictionary."*
>
> – Vince Lombardi

moral to the story, for rarely does going slowly win any races. Going slowly is a good way to be careful, but that's not what races are about. In fact, the real lesson is not about the tortoise at all; it's about the hare.

The hare believes that he's faster than the tortoise, and he's right. In a typical race, the hare will beat the tortoise every time. But the hare makes a huge mistake, believing in his ability but then not actually proving it. You may have great skill, one which everyone acknowledges, but you must still use that skill in competition to actually win competition. Overconfidence that leads to a lackadaisical attitude will often be punished by embarrassing failure. While it is true that somebody with less skills but who works his ass off will sometimes beat out somebody lazy with lots of skills, the real lesson here is that you must use your abilities when they are called upon. If we learn anything from the tortoise, it is that when you are faced with an opponent who will certainly defeat you, the only hope you have is that he defeats himself. The correct moral: success depends on using your talents, not just having them.[4]

Look at it this way, let's say you have two people competing for a race. One person has come from a long line of successful runners, has always excelled in sports and has been running throughout his or her entire life. Then look at another person who does not come from a line of winners, but instead, this person has worked hard from the start, always struggling but never giving up.

The latter person, although lacking in natural talent, has a determination and a drive like no other. She wakes at 4 a.m., trains six days a week and hires one of the best trainers. Meanwhile, the 'naturally talented' person might get up at 7 to train for the race and only train during the work week. The underdog, so to speak, is working harder and putting more effort and focus into the whole thing, and therefore, she's likely to beat the girl with talent. At this point, talent no longer is in her favor. The girl who gets up at 4 a.m. six days a week has 21 more hours of practice and training than the naturally talented runner, therefore, changing the odds of the race.

Many talented people have wasted their gifts and just not worked hard to enhance themselves. These types of people might be famous and well known, but in the long run and the bigger picture, they fade into the background when really skillful, hard working people come on the scene. It boils down to your work ethic and how much effort you're willing to put into something. As many people know, in life, you get what you put into it, so if you've got something you're aiming for, something you want to do, work hard and you'll create a lasting legacy, or at the very least, an unexpected victory.

Talent is sometimes thought of as a gift, having an aptitude that's a cut above the rest. It allows an individual to really excel at the activity in question, but talent doesn't always come naturally. By working hard, people can develop talent and what seems to be a gift is, in fact, just the result of working REALLY hard for a long time. Many famous people are famous not because they have had 'overnight success' but because, behind the scenes, they have been working really hard.

Journey to Amazing

Develop your talent by working hard. The more work you put into something, the more you'll get out of it. Although you may not have a natural 'talent' or aptitude for it initially, in time, with focus and hard work, you'll become a master. One becomes a master through repetition, faith and hard work. You must master your craft in order for it to be a worthy gift to share with the world. A simple way to start is to get motivated and inspired. Motivation is the first step in achieving great success, for a motivated mind is a highly energized mind that can be taken in any direction. Motivation comes from the outside in, and incentives and motives are often used to impale. Determine rewards for accomplishing a goal. This gives you incentive to keep striving. Most times, one gets excited about something initially, and then the feelings subside after a short period of time. That's great to get you started, but inspiration is what keeps you going. Unlike motivation, inspiration, on the other hand, comes from the inside out. You know when one is inspired when you have a burning sense of desire that resides within you and a commitment to persist until the challenges are overcome and the goal is reached. Hard work requires dedication and perseverance. You must be ready, willing and able. Without commitment, you'll never start, and without consistency, you never finished.

Each day, write a "commitment pledge." This means you must commit to whatever you write. You may want to share this with those closest to you (i.e. people in your household or at work) in order to have some accountability. A commitment pledge consists of an *I am* statement and an *I will* statement. Here are examples:

I am focused, so *I will* complete all my work today.

I am reliable, so *I will* be on time everywhere I go today.

I am giving, so *I will* cut my elderly neighbor's grass today.

After successfully completing a pledge for one day, extend it to two days and then a week, and so forth. Keep extending the pledge until you the behavior becomes second nature.

6.

NEVER SETTLING FOR BEING GOOD

Many people have audacious aspirations and bold dreams, but they end up settling for good instead of great. We feel passable because although we may not have reached our potential, at least we're not bad. In most cases, just being good is the easy way out. It may not take a lot of initiative, creativity, passion and courage. The praise and reward for being better or "not as bad as" the person in the cubicle next to you gives us a false sense of security. It quiets us, deadens us and seduces us into thinking that we don't really need to try. That's why good is the enemy of great.

> *"If better is possible, good is not enough."*
> – Benjamin Franklin

In fact, I suspect 'good' is worse than 'bad'. Everyone understands bad, poor, below average and 'not good enough'. 'Bad' practically shouts, "Change!" Meanwhile 'good' whispers, 'Stay the same.' Jim Collins, author of the book *Good to Great*, says that one of the key reasons why we have so little that become great is because the vast majority have become quite good. If good represents mediocrity, sameness, getting by and 'good enough,' then it certainly is the enemy of greatness, excellence, high standards and 'going above and beyond'.

Contentment with being "good" gives you no burning need to change. Once you stop comparing your successes or failures to others or when you realize that your only competition is in the mirror and you truly believe that the world needs your greatness, you will be moved to action. The world has too many good people and not enough great ones. Think for a moment, what if Martin Luther King Jr. or Nelson Mandela had settled for just being good? Greatness changes the world while being good merely treads water.

I'm sure we have many things that we do well, but what is it that you do great? Most often, the things that you do well are those you have been trained or taught to do. These may also be skills that you've mastered through repitition. However, great appears and feels differently. Your greatness comes naturally without training and experience. It's the one or the few complementary things you can do better or more uniquely than anyone else can. Yes, you may still get coaching to get even better, but no one had to develop your core ability or talent. It was already there.

While most people focus on entertainment-related talents, such as singing and acting, because they are so obvious and exciting, greatness also comes in the form of simple gifts that we may overlook. Being naturally sympathetic or caring is useful in ministerial and counseling fields, for instance. Having a love and knack for growing plants can easily lead to a career in landscaping, horticulture and so forth. The point is that the greatness of your modest ability is sufficient for your role or purpose in this world. You may never end up on a stage or standing before a crowd, but you will be content and so, too, will be those who connect to your greatness.

It may be difficult to recognize the difference between your good and greatness. One easy way to recognize it is your good will get you wings but not cause you to fly. However, your great will cause you to soar. This means you will be an eagle rather than an ostrich or even a chicken. Things that cause you to fly are the universe's way of drawing you closer to your purpose, and you cannot truly have greatness unless it includes your life-calling.

Few people will attain great lives because it's so easy to settle for a good life. I have a friend who is one of the smartest and most talented people I know. I often go to her for business advice, creative ideas and support. She is hyper-educated from some of the top schools in the country, and she does pretty "good" for herself. Nevertheless, she wakes up every day and goes to a job that makes her miserable. It doesn't challenge her, feed her passion or ignite her soul. To those on the outside, she would appear to have a "good life," which is easy and comfortable. Renowned motivational speaker Les Brown, counters that notion by saying, "If you do what is easy, your life will be hard." Life is hard for her because she's trading hours for dollars. The gloomiest part is that she knows that she has greatness in some other vocation, but fear leads her to retain her miserable sufficiency. As I like to say, "There is no greater agony than bearing an untold story inside you."

Several years ago, I found myself in that same place. I worked for a company for 14 years. That's 5,110 days, or 122,640 hours. While I had an impressive title and made a decent living, it was not my life's purpose. Each year, I reminded myself that I'd never retire from a company. There was an uncomfortable feeling that I had, knowing that I could do better. No matter what I did, that feeling of wanting something more fulfilling would never subside. I wrote my resignation letter countless times but never submitted it. Finally, on February 14th, I chose love over fear, and I resigned 14 years to the exact date I started. I knew that this time I had to take a leap of faith. Something in me was pulling me, and if I didn't answer the calling, I would upset the natural order of my universe and miss my greatness.

Over the next year, I sought out on a journey to find my amazing. I opened my private counseling practice and "turned pro," as I like to call it. Pros seek greatness, but amateurs settle for being good. Within a year, I made more money in four months than I had earned in a year's salary on my job. More importantly, though, I was able to use my gifts to help people help themselves and change the world. I was only able to do this because I was operating in my greatness.

It's quite easy for us to recognize greatness in others. We can plainly see their gifts and talents, and we even encourage them to follow their passion and dreams. However, when it comes to us identifying our own greatness, it can be difficult. Some misguided people even believe they are great at many things. We've often heard the saying, "Jack of all trades but master of none." We may find ourselves being good, not great, at many things, but in doing this, we miss our opportunity to discover our greatness. A few pats on the back or a couple hundred social media "Likes" can give us a false sense of achievement in things we are only good at doing.

Furthermore, we tend to get a bit uncomfortable, shy and suddenly have a loss for words when discussing our greatness. Perhaps this is because of fear of judgment or maybe it's because we've been taught that it is not polite to brag. We avoid talking about our own amazing talents in an effort not to seem vain or arrogant. My mom would say, "It's a sad dog that won't wag his own tail." What that simply means is that you have the right to talk openly about your ability or gifting, and in fact, if you don't, then who will? Denying your greatness keeps you in the "good" place. In order to really accept your greatness, you must shout your talent to the world. While humbleness may be a virtue, rejecting or down-playing your God-given gift is sinful. There is a huge difference between acknowledging your greatness and being arrogant. Arrogance screams, "My talent is better than yours!" Acknowledging your greatness says, "I am great because we all have greatness!"

If it's that easy to follow your passion and move to greatness, why don't most people do it? At one point, fear led both my friend and me. Fear keeps you hostage and robs you of your greatness. It is only when I began to publicly acknowledge my greatness and give love to my gifting, that they began to work for me. No one said it would be easy, but it will be worth it ultimately. Don't be afraid to give up the good to go for the great. Remember, your life shrinks or expands directly in proportion to your courage, according to poet Anais Nin.

Everyone has greatness within him or her. As the saying goes, "Stop waiting for the world to recognize your greatness, live it and let the world catch up to you." Maybe you think getting to the next level requires having more resources, such as money or personnel. However, greatness depends not on what you have to work with, but on what you choose to do with it. The next unit focuses on faith, which is the main resource you'll need to move from okay to AMAZING!

Journey to Amazing

Think of what your life would be like if you operated in your greatness. Think about some of the most successful people you know. What is the one thing that makes them great or special? What makes great people great? There is truly a formula. They all have similar characteristics, such as courage and confidence. Look at people you know who are operating in their greatness. Write down their traits beyond just talent or skill. What similarities do you have with them? Begin to compare and contrast. Truly successful people find other more successful people to model and imitate. There is no need to reinvent the wheel. You can learn from others' experiences and mistakes. According to motivational speaker Tony Robbins, "If you want to be successful, find someone who has achieved the results you want and copy what they do and you'll achieve the same results." As you uncover these secrets to success and incorporate them in your life, never lose what already makes you special. Therefore, find a successful person's approach to what you seek to achieve and add their formula into what you're already doing.

7.

YOUR WORDS ARE YOU

Our words are powerful creators of our lives. Most know the late Mohammed Ali as a champion professional boxer. He has been called the "greatest of all time" (GOAT). He is also known for his quick wit, as well as his quick hands. What I liked most about Mohammed Ali was his positive self-talk. One of the things that he said that always stood out was: "To be a great champion, you must believe that you are the best. Even if you're not, pretend that you are." Ali went on to say, at one point, "that what you are thinking about you become." Your thoughts affect your words and your actions are inspired by your words.

> *"Your words will tell others what you think. Your actions will tell what you believe."*
>
> – T.D. Jakes

We've all seen the picture with the glass half full of water and the question is do you see the glass half full or half empty? It's all about how you think, the way you look at it. The person who sees the glass as half-empty is a pessimist, and the one who sees it as half-full is an optimist. In fact, optimism is the key to positive thinking. Optimism comes from the Latin word *optimus*, meaning "best," which describes how an optimistic person is always looking for the best in every situation and expecting good things to happen. In a nutshell, optimism is the tendency to believe, expect or to hope that things turn out well.

Winston Churchill said, "A pessimist sees the difficulty in every opportunity; an optimist sees opportunity in every difficulty." It's just that easy. One of the first steps is to believe that a positive attitude is a choice. I've found that this is one of the most difficult steps to take in the beginning for my clients. It is difficult because it's hard to tell people that "you've made a choice to think negatively instead positively." It becomes more believable when they can make the connection with the choices that they've made. I believe Ali says it best: "It's the repetition of affirmations that leads to belief, and once that belief becomes a deep conviction, things begin to happen."

Ridding your life of negativity is easier said than done, but if you want to live a more positive, joyful life, negative people who don't encourage your happiness cannot surround you. When you are a negative person, you attract negativity, those who reinforce your pessimistic belief system because that's the vibrational frequency you are on. When you change your frequency and you move those negative things and people out of your life, then you begin to realize that positivity is a choice and declare, "I decide what I think, say and am."

This does not mean that negative, difficult situations do not continue to happen all around you. It's that you aren't on the vibrational frequency to see them anymore. You cannot expect to have a positive life with a negative mindset. Thus, reinforce the positivity in your life. Once you start thinking more positively, then you will realize how to reinforce your thoughts and your behavior.

How we feel about ourselves is directly influenced by what we think about ourselves. The power of positive thinking can think you into happiness and totally improve your life. The power of thought is really important to me as a cognitive behavior therapist. I know that your thoughts affect her behavior. If you change your thoughts, you change your behavior, which can ultimately change your life.

Words vs. Action

Have you noticed that your actions can have greater impact than your words? Sometimes you don't even have to say anything to impact someone. What we think is how we see ourselves, what we say is who we want to be, but what we do is truly who we are. I was working with a group of educators who had grown frustrated with some of the students. On one of the boards was the Chinese proverb: "Tell me and I forget; teach me and I may remember; involve me and I learn." I asked them what they thought that quote meant. They gave me several responses and one teacher stated, "Actions speak louder than words!" That was precisely correct. What better way to help them understand than to involve the students? So, we tested the action cliché. My goal was to prove that people do actually learn better through involvement than through words. My subjects were two pre-K classes (age group: 4-5 year-old boys and girls).

The goal was to get the children to cleanup the classroom properly, putting everything in its place in a neat, orderly fashion. The teacher in Classroom 1 only gave instructions. She explained exactly where the books were to go, where the paint went, how to clean the paintbrushes, how to stack the blocks, etc. The teacher in Classroom 2 showed them the exact place of each toy, how to stack them, how to clean the paintbrushes, and so forth. The teacher did this without saying anything in the process, only giving them a brief introduction of what she was doing. After doing this three times, Classroom 2 was significantly cleaner than Classroom 1, proving that actions speak louder than words. I've done this type of exercise with adults, and the results have been the same each time.

Self-Ta lk

When you say something in a curt or rude manner, people will typically become defensive. When you are friendly and gracious, people will want to help. The same is true for the way we speak to ourselves. Negative self-talk will yield negative results, and positive self-talk will yield positive results.

Think about this how many times throughout the day you say I am tired; I am broke; I am sick; I am sad; I am lonely; I am mad; or I am over it. There is a significant amount of power in these "I AM" statements. In fact, "I am" is the most powerful phrase that you will ever speak in terms of shaping your future or changing her life.

If the words "I am" have an especially strong creative power, what is it that we're telling ourselves daily? Every time we use the words "I am," you are calling in the Divine Power to act on whatever you are proclaiming. Pay attention the next time you say something like "I am tired" and watch what kind of feelings follow. You begin to be a little bit lethargic and your energy level drops simply because you have told the universe that this is who you are. Again, you must understand how important "I am" statements are in shaping your day and destiny.

With the positive self-talk, including I am statements, you're pumping yourself up to say and believe, "I am worthy of receiving the best in life. I am a champion. I am a creator. I am resourceful. I am successful." As you begin to believe your "I am" statements, this directly affects your "I can." So, for instance, once you believe that "I am good with money," you begin to be that. You begin to believe that it is possible for you to do it.

My daughter, Temple, was getting ready to take a third grade standardized test. Where we live, in order to be promoted to the fourth grade, you must pass this standardized test. One day, one of her homework assignments was to read and initial a list of "I can" statements that her teacher had given her. The "I can" statements were actually an assessment for the teachers to see what it is the students can do and identify the areas that students may need more instructional support. Temple's "I can" math statements included everything from "I can use multiplication to check my division" to "I can divide a whole into four parts." Whatever it was that she declared she could do, directly correlated with her "I am" statements. In other words, it was like saying, "If you believe that I am not good enough, then you don't really think I can pass this test." This leads me to "I will" statements. All of your "I" statements work together, in fact. "I am" allows you to believe that "I can," and your "I can" will directly support your "I will." Once you're sure about your "I am," then you know that you can. For example, when declaring,

"I am awesome," then I know that "I can" do awesome things. I can do things that are extraordinary. I can do things that nobody believed I could. I can do things I didn't believe I could.

"I will" is a key factor. It's not can you do it, but it's will you do it. Once you set yourself up to having a positive outlook on life and believe that you can, then your next step of action is "I will…" It may look as if some people are born with superpowers, but really, their only superpower is that they just don't quit. That's the "will" part in action. A popular saying goes: "Behind me is infinite power. Before me endless possibilities. Around me is boundless opportunities." You have to believe and remind yourself of this on a daily basis.

Journey to Amazing

Get a blank sheet of paper and pen, and then stand in front of the mirror. Look yourself in the eye and say "I am…." (finish the statement). Write it down. Look at yourself again and say that "I am..." Repeat this process over the next 10 to 15 minutes. It's going to be a bit uncomfortable if you are not used to saying "I am" statements. Once you complete this list, I want you to go back and review it. What you're looking for now is to see if there's any negative or any limiting "I am" statements (i.e. I am dumb; I am lazy; I am too small). I want you to cross out all the negative or limiting statements. Wait, I don't want you to just cross them out; I want you to take your pen and scratch them out furiously. Put some anger into it and some disgust behind it. Make sure they are completely blacked out so you can't ever read them again. The goal is to seriously remove these limiting, negative statements from your mind.

Now you should be left with a list of these things that are positive or promising about you. This may seem a bit silly, but I recommend reading them aloud and saying them with enthusiasm. I want you to do it with lots of energy. You can wave your hands in the air, dance around and pump your fist. This type of celebration is going to get you excited about celebrating the positive things that you are. If you aren't accustomed to doing "I am" statements, I really want you to do this exercise about two to three times a day. Notice how your mood shifts and how it changes. Once you know your "I am's," you can begin to move in the mindset of "I can." Next, what *will* you do? Because I'm sure you can do anything, but what is it that you are willing to do?

UNIT 3
KEEPING THE FAITH

Preparation

Vision Amazing Faith

Gratitude

Dreams don't have a size limit or a deadline, and the great news is there is no expiration date. What if it takes you 15 years for your dream to come true? What if you're age 45 and just starting on your journey? The average person lives to be 65 years old. Therefore, you have a lifetime to explore what makes you happy while honoring your calling and uncovering your purpose. Most people get caught up in watching the clock and putting expirations on themselves because society says that you're supposed to graduate high school by 18 years, college by 22, and be married with kids by 30. Dreams are like fingerprints, for they are all different. If a person still has a heartbeat, there is still time for a dream.

We may fail sometimes, but this absolutely does not mean that we will fail every time. Thomas Edison, one of the most famous inventors in the 20th century, tried more than one thousand times before he found out that tungsten was the right material for the electric light bulb. His determination was like that of most great scientists. JK Rowling reminds us that we are to decide for ourselves what constitutes failure, but

> *"For every disadvantage, there is a corresponding advantage."*
> – W. Clement Stone

the world is quite eager to give us a set of criteria if we allow it. Zig Ziglar famously said, "Failure is an event, not a person."

It's not likely to achieve great success on the first try. Thus, success is always based on a great deal of failure. For instance, when physicists and couple Pierre and Marie Curie faced failures, they never gave up and always told themselves to stick to what they were doing. They discovered polonium and radium in 1898. Then the Curies and scientist Henri Becquerel won a Nobel Prize for Physics in 1903 for discovering radioactivity.

Psychologists say that the influence of what we strongly believe is important to our career success. First, we have to make sure that our goal is achievable and practical. Then we must pursue it no matter how difficult it is. How does one persevere through difficulties even when the goal is noble? The answer is faith. Even if it is one ounce of hope, that is enough to fuel our journey to amazing. We simply cannot, at any cost, lose all hope if we ever expect to realize our dream.

8.

HOPE AS THE FOUNDATION

Hope is faith in seed form. Faith is hope in final form. In 2004, Barak Obama evoked the power of hope when he addressed the Democratic National Convention, stating:

In the end, that's what this election is about. Do we participate in a politics of cynicism or a politics of hope? John Kerry calls on us to hope. John Edwards calls on us to hope. I'm not talking about blind optimism here — the almost willful ignorance that thinks unemployment will go away if we just don't talk about it, or the health care crisis will solve itself if we just ignore it. No, I'm talking about something more substantial. It's the hope of slaves sitting around a fire singing freedom songs; the hope of immigrants setting out for distant shores; the hope of a young naval lieutenant bravely patrolling the Mekong Delta; the hope of a millworker's son who dares to defy the odds; the hope of a skinny kid with a funny name who believes that America has a place for him, too. Hope in the face of difficulty. Hope in the face of uncertainty.

In 2006, then Illinois Senator Barack Obama wrote the book

"The Audacity of Hope: Thoughts on Reclaiming the American Dream." It quickly became a *New York Times* best-seller, and ultimately, its ideology became part of his mantra in his 2008 presidential campaign. That message of hope resonated with the electorate, and he became the 44th president of the United States, following his dream all the way to the White House.

Every dream has the possibility of becoming a reality. Its manifestation, however, is contingent upon how much you really believe. One of the buzzwords of Obama's speech wasn't merely hope, but also "audacity." When one is audacious, he or she is bold and brave. Some may consider it luck or America's desperation for change, but it definitely took great courage to believe that he could become the first black president of the United States of America.

It has been said, "Fortune favors he who is prepared to follow his dream, for a dream was never given without the potential to come true." Some people may get a lucky break, but through my research, those who have made their dreams come true, do so with sacrifice, sweat and tears. Luck is when preparation meets opportunity. Luck is not in your hands but decisions are. Your decisions can make you seem lucky, but luck can never diminish the power of your decisions.

You may have experienced crushing defeats and terrifying situations that you couldn't change or control that caused you to lose hope. As a result, you began to play the "blame game," blaming others and even blaming yourself. Then the power of self-fulfilling prophecy kicks in, and because your beliefs and actions are congruent, you begin to perceive everything as negative and despair about life in general. You've punctuated your life with a period after defeat rather than a semicolon. The period denotes "the end" while a semicolon is used when an author could've chosen to end a sentence but chose to continue it. A semicolon says it's not over yet. There is still hope. In times of despair, the one thing that helps us carry on and continue to fight is hope. Hope gives us options, believing in unforeseen possibilities. And what we know for sure is that if it is possible for someone else, then it is possible for us too.

We all have the ability to develop hope. We don't have to buy or borrow it, for we already have it. You can uncover hope by simply reflecting on life's possibilities. During times of hope-lessness or uncertainty, think about and compare past feelings, situations, outcomes, options, and possibilities. Remember when similar moments in your life existed, how

> *"Hope is being able to see that there is light despite all of the darkness."*
> – Desmond Tutu

you dealt with the situation and was finally able to move on past it. In every situation that you have overcome, hope was the common denominator. For example, recall when someone you really liked or loved broke your heart, but at some point, you were able to get over it. When anything similar occurs again, you can be hopeful that you can overcome this new situation too.

Have you ever done a visualization or imagery exercise? Perhaps, you imagined you were on a beach. You felt the heat of the sun on your face, felt the sensation of sand sliding through your toes, relaxed to the sounds of the waves, and smelled fresh ocean air. When the exercise was over, you recalled feeling like you were actually at the beach. That is the power of the mind! You can actually bring your past or anticipated experiences and feelings into the present. Therefore, you can produce hope by focusing on joyous moments that you have experienced or you can bring about hope by imagining the future as you dream it to be. This allows you to create hope that brings forth a feeling of expectation and desire for a particular thing to happen.

Your dreams are ideas or visions that are created in your imagination. Although they are not real – at least not immediately – they are something that you have wanted very much to do, be or have for a long time. Simply put, if you can imagine it, it's possible. Some may say your aspiration is impossible until it's done. This is what happened with 19-year-old Gertrude Ederle. After failing once in 1926, she became the first woman to swim the 21 miles from Dover, England, to Cape Griz-Nez across the English Channel, which separates Great Britain from the north-western tip of France. Afterward, Ederle told Alec Rutherford of *The New York Times,* "I knew it could be done, it had to be done, and I did it."[5] She offered these words of encouragement when asked what made her reach her goal this time, "Never, never give up because I can always see the coast, and it brings me courage all the time." She went on to say that she chose a very sunny day to make sure that she could see her hope materialize, so she just went for it.

In psychology, we talk about the Flight, Freeze or Fight Response, sometimes called the "acute stress response." It reminds me a lot of the "give in, give up or give it all you've got" concept. The term "fight or flight" describes a mechanism in the body that enables humans and animals to mobilize a lot of energy rapidly in order to cope with threats to survival. What's important about this response is that it operates on "hope," the hope that in imminent danger you can either out run (flight) the threat or you can win (fight) in battle against the perceived threat. Most recently added to this response is "freeze." It is very similar to the "give in" response, choosing not to act either way but still hoping that the lack of response will have a good outcome.

We all have choices in life. In fact, our supreme existence is based on our ability to reason and to make choices. Our overall happiness and success in life all boils down to the choices we make. For instance, you may decide to pursue a college degree instead of a music career; you may choose a career over having a family; or you may decide to leave a relationship instead of fighting for it. This life's journey is full of tough choices that ultimately will shape our future. What I've realized is that it all comes down to three choices: You can give in, give up or give it all you've got.

When you don't believe that your opinion matters and that you can't make a difference, this yields a sense of hopelessness. With that expectation, you go with the masses or the popular vote. You conform or you just give in. Only dead fish go with the flow. You have to dare to be different. It takes no effort on the part of a fish to go with the flow and drift downstream. All you have to do is just float and that's easy. However, to travel upstream in the direction of your dreams takes some courage.

There is a big difference between being alive and living. Being alive is simply breathing; living involves taking someone's breath away. Once you make a decision to throw in the towel, do nothing, set aside your talent to watch your dreams fade and become distant memories, you've given up on life. When you cease making an effort or resign yourself to failure, the game is over.

The choice of champions is to give it all you've got! This is what separates winners and history-makers. When you give it all you've got, you show up every time. Some people talk about what happened, others wonder what happened, while a few people make things happen. Learn to be great right where you are and give everything you've got every time. It doesn't mean that your goal is to stay there, it means that you honor the opportunity that you've been given at the time, investing every fiber of your being and using every resource, every lesson, everything. You're all in.

As previously noted, we all have choices. Where you are in your life adds up to be the sum of your choices. Hope is one of the strongest forces in the universe. It is a feeling of expectation and desire for a certain outcome. When hope influences your decisions or choices, you operate with an optimistic attitude that is based on an expectation of positive outcomes. However, it is great to expect to make a million dollars in a year, but have the choices you've made add up to that result. Giving in (freeze) will possibly get you there if you ride the wave of others who are calling the shots for your life. Giving up (flight) will give you no chance because you've decided to quit. However, giving it all you've got (fight) says that I have a goal, or mission, and I'm going to do whatever it takes to accomplish it.

No matter what, hold on to your dreams. Don't lose ever lose hope, for it has a sustaining power as long as we believe.

Journey to Amazing

Hope, sometimes that's all you have when you have nothing else, but if you have it, then you actually have everything. During our most difficult times, through failures, sadness and even despair, having hope for the future and believing things are going to be better goes beyond just repeating affirmations. You must remember to dream. There is a strong connection between dreams and hope. Remembering your dreams can improve your mood and help you become more hopeful. In fact, dreams resuscitate hope. That said, find a space where there are no distractions. Think about the dreams you had long ago or create new ones if you don't have any. Write them down. Read your dreams aloud daily. The goal is to program your subconscious to believe in them. This fosters hope. Once your subconscious mind sees a possible dream, it automatically believes that there is hope and the likelihood of a better future. Be sure not to confuse this with daydreaming. The difference is that daydreams distract people from reality. They're used to escape, while a dream motivates you to move toward a new reality.

9.

CONFRONTING FEAR

Fear is the opposite of faith. The paradox is that both fear and faith make us uncomfortable. However, only one is freeing. The other is enslaving. When you want someone to remain stagnant or feel powerless, invoke fear. On the other hand, encourage and inspire people beyond what they believe they are capable of, and most will at least try to succeed in faith.

Fear is natural mechanism that works to make us feel safe and protected. However, we often misuse it and overly rely on it. You'll hear people use their fears as a reason for inaction or even regression. Here are some common fears:

Fear of rejection or ridicule
Fear of loss
Fear of the unknown
Fear of failure
Fear of loneliness
Fear of death

Fear occurs as a response to something that is perceived as being threatening, dangerous or harmful. Fear causes a person to feel nervous, anxious and even impairs bodily functions by interfering with the ability to think or speak clearly. An article in *Psychology Today* gave a great working definition of fear. It explained that fear is a vital response to physical and emotional danger, and it also explained that if we did not feel fear, we couldn't protect ourselves from legitimate threats. However, oftentimes, we fear situations that are far from life-threatening, becoming defensive or fighting for unnecessary reasons.

We are born with only two fears: loud noises and falling. So, if you were not born with the fears that you currently have today, where did they come from? You acquired them in response to *perceived* or *actual* danger, negativity, rejection, and failure. At some point in your life, you associated pain or risk with a particular experience, so you try to avoid any similar situations. Fear then becomes a mechanism to help you avoid potentially negative experiences. For instance, a young boy declares his feelings for a classmate in a handwritten note that he hid in his notebook. Somehow, the note falls out and another student finds it. Rather than return the note, the student reads the note aloud during lunch. Embarrassed, the boy tries to physically grab the note from the student. The two begin to tussle before an adult notices and intervenes. Both of them get in trouble, but more importantly, the boy's object of affection, laughs at him. Later on in his life, he never expressed his feelings to any other woman he liked. He feared rejection, something he felt as a young boy when he shared his feelings.

So if you acquired most of your fears, this means they are

> *"Confront your fears, list them, get to know them, and only then will you be able to put them aside and move ahead."*
>
> — Desmond Tutu

learned behaviors. The good news is that anything you learn can be unlearned. First, you need to understand your fears: the cause and the cures. As I mentioned earlier, fears and other emotions allow us to avoid or escape unwanted situations. This would certainly be helpful if a lion was stalking you in a jungle, but more often than not, fear stops us from doing things that we want or need to do. In fact, you probably are in constant battle with your fears every day.

It is important for us to know how fear works. For instance, you get scared before you do a parachute jump out of an airplane, not afterward. This is why fear is so dangerous. The greatest things you can achieve in life are scary, but nothing will happen if you just sit on your sofa all day, staying in your comfort zone[6]. In a nutshell, think of fear as being similar to some medicines. The most effective medications often have unwanted, unintended side effects. Similarly, it's the side effects of fear that you need to overcome. These include stagnation, denial, and low self-esteem. How do you overcome this? Quite simply, you destroy fear and its effects by first recognizing the fear itself. If you don't know what scares you, then you can never do anything about it.

All fears come down to three main types: internal, external and subconscious. External fears are caused by something outside of you. Traumatic past events typically trigger them. This is when someone fears something specific, such as flying, spiders, and the number 13. For instance, if a bee stung you at a young age, you may develop a phobia of bees. Your experience taught you to avoid them. External fears are easily recognized. Past situations can also cause internal fears. However, internal fears are persistent emotional states that are not specific to any circumstance. This can make these fears difficult to recognize. Internal fears manifest as: fear of failure, fear of success, fear of rejection, and self-doubt. Having a fear of failure, for example, can stop someone from starting her own business or asking someone out on a date. Internal fears are especially critical because they can make you think that this is just who you are rather than fear driving it. Essentially, these fears can really hold you back in life. Although we are not fully aware of them, subconscious fears are so potent that we develop beliefs around them. These fears develop into limiting beliefs, and limited beliefs filter into how we see the world. They influence our actions and feelings. An example of a limiting belief would be if you believe you will never find a satisfying job because every job you had was terrible. Limiting beliefs usually try to convince you that you are not good enough or even that some types of people or places are not good at all. Because they form beliefs, subconscious fears are difficult to recognize and eliminate.

You wouldn't believe the extent that irrational beliefs can affect your life and your ability to move forward. You have to realize that beliefs are not facts. How many beliefs have you had that you came to realize are not true? Sometimes what you think about yourself is an irrational belief. I spend a great deal of time in my practice first helping clients realize how extreme and irrational their generalized beliefs are sometimes. Then I discuss how more rational, useful beliefs can help change their situation, and from that, I help them adopt more reasonable, functional beliefs that can render them long-term success.

Many fears are caused by ignorance because people are scared of what they don't know. The reason for this is simple. Your brain only gives you a few pieces of information and tends to fill in the rest of the details by itself. For example, when you look at your computer screen, what you're actually seeing is a series of tiny dots. However, because the dots are so small, your brain fills in the gaps so you can see a complete picture. That's the exact same principle that applies when it comes to fear. If you start thinking about something for which you don't have all the information, your brain will fill in the gaps. Before you know it, you are imagining things that may never have happened or have no chance of happening. Take, for instance, a situation where someone either never returns your call or message. You may not hastily begin to deduce reasons for this, but in time, you will. Some people may come think the reason for this is something personal (e.g. "he/she doesn't like me"), while others may believe there was some third party influence (e.g. "he/she never got the message because…").

So in order to stand the best chance of overcoming your fear, you need to find out as much as you can about your fear. This way, you'll be able to react on the basis of complete information rather than incomplete information. In turn, this will prevent you from worrying about things that you shouldn't worry about. It will also help you to reduce the level of fear that you experience by making you aware of exactly what happened rather than making you imagine or guess what might happen.

For every fear, certain things are driving or amplifying that fear. If you are afraid of flying, you're probably not afraid of planes; what you're really afraid of is the plane crashing and you dying as a result. To overcome a fear, you need to identify the drivers of that fear and then systematically work to eliminate them one by one. The more drivers you eliminate, the weaker your fear will become, reducing your anxiety, apprehension and terror. So how do you ultimately get over these fears? After you recognize them, you must confront them. I repeat, in order to overcome your fears, you must confront them head on. There is no other way.

In confronting any type of learned fear, you must reprogram your inappropriate fight or flight response. This means you must purposely do things that frighten you. When you are scared, an automatic reaction of resistance and anxiety occur. You don't even have to consciously think about the feeling; it just happens. Your body reacts with an increased heart rate, breathing and muscle tension so you know to defend yourself. This built-in survival mechanism called the "flight or fight" response is hard-wired into our DNA. This is why your reaction can occur without you even consciously thinking about.

Whenever you're presented with the fear – no matter how big or small – your survival mechanism kicks in because it thinks that you need to be protected from some type of danger. Now how do you reprogram your flight or fight response? Again, confronting your fears is the only way. This means you must intentionally subject yourself to the very thing that you fear. Maybe you will have to begin small and then work yourself up to bigger challenges, but you must begin to confront the fear. Change your response to the fear as you confront it. You can, for instance, learn to laugh at your fear. This is what comedian Kevin Hart learned to do, and he became successful from doing it through comedy. Perhaps you are taking yourself too seriously, thinking that your issue is the worst there ever was or that no one else could ever understand. These are examples of irrational limiting beliefs confounded by subconscious fears. There is no situation on Earth that is exclusive to one person, and more than likely, there is someone worse off than you. Grammy Award-winning gospel singer Kirk Franklin actually penned a song to his fears ("Hello Fear"), bidding them farewell because he was "tired of being brokenhearted." He wanted back what fear had taken from him, singing:

All my hopes and my dreams you took from me
I want those back before you leave

You will know when you overcome your fears, or at least have control of them to a manageable level, because your body will remain calm when exposed to the thing that you dislike or have tried to avoid. This is a sign that you have reprogrammed your inappropriate fight or flight response. It is important not to expect an inappropriate flight or fight response to switch off instantly, as it could take many repeated exposures to your fear before it slowly starts to dissipate. The goal is to become desensitized to your fears. When the strength of your fears decrease, the more command you will have over your life and choices. Systematic desensitization is actually a type of behavioral therapy. I use this type of therapy to remove the fear response of a phobia to substitute it with a relaxation response.

Here is a simple systematic exercise that you can do yourself. First, I have the client form a hierarchy of different fears. Next, I give a training session on relaxation, showing them how to control their breathing and release tension through meditation. In this step, they learn to relax when presented with their fear, for it is impossible to be both relaxed and anxious at the same time. Finally, my clients are presented with their fears according to the hierarchy they had documented. Thus, I start with the lesser ones and build up to the greater fears. Of course, if you're terrified of spiders, I'm not going to put a tarantula on your arm. We would start with maybe something as simple as a picture of someone looking at a spider at the zoo or seeing a spider on television. Then I use the relaxation techniques to control their anxiety so they are able to lessen their anxiety when confronted with their fears.

Basically, we must identify, confront and let go of our fears in order to attain our dreams. Always remember, fear has killed more dreams than failure ever will. Les Brown says it best: "So many of us are not living our dreams because we are living out fears." Each of us experience times when we are afraid. Fear has a legitimate function in our lives. It alerts us to things that could possibly be harmful to us. Most of the time, we are able to evaluate the situation, determine if the danger is real and deal with it. Other times, our fear gets the best of us and interferes with our daily living. Don't let fear rob you of your dreams, steal your joy, and deny you of living your best life.

Journey to Amazing

Describe circumstances or people who have triggered your desire to give up. Determine what about those situations scared you. Monitor your self-talk. What are you saying to yourself that scares you? Visualize yourself still being afraid but handling the situation in an acceptable manner. Then gradually expose yourself to the feared situation by doing things that more and more closely approximate what you fear.

10.

USING YOUR 'WHY'

When you have a good reason, you'll find a way. My undergraduate college motto at Clark Atlanta University was "Find a Way or Make One." I eventually came to learn, firsthand, what that meant. I once complained to my department chair about another professor, and I knew that I was absolutely right. I knew the department chair knew I was right as well. She asked, "What can you do?" I then proceeded to run down a long list of things I could have done to end up with a favorable result. I wasn't pleased at the time, but I got the lesson. I could not have both excuses and results. My "why" was that I was going to be the first person in my immediate family to graduate from college. The "how" was by any means necessary.

> *"The two most important days in your life are the day you are born and the day you find out why."*
>
> – Mark Twain

German philosopher Frederick Nietzsche said, "He who has a why can endure anyhow." Knowing your "why" is the single most important step to figuring out how. Your why has to be something that that inspires you, that's a critical part of your existence. It is integrated into your soul's purpose. Your "why" is a cause that is bigger than you are, and it is consistent with *who* you are and what you care about. When you know your why, you will stay motivated even when the odds are against you. You will find the bravery to take the necessary risks. My "why" went way beyond just a diploma. I've been a therapist since 4th grade, literally. I remember playing at P.E. and giving good advice, coming up with logical solutions for others' problems and healing their sadness.   So, this is not just my career, but also my soul calling, my life's purpose. Growing up in inner city Atlanta, in one of the highest crime and school dropout zones, the odds were certainly against me. Statistically, I was not supposed to make it out of high school, let alone go to college. When you know that there is a bigger calling on your life, though, you will defy the odds and weather the storms to risk it all.

An easy way to figure out your why is to find where you add value. This is not about what you are good at doing. Many people do work that they are good at but they loathe. Education, training and experience can help you be good at most anything, but does it provide fulfillment? So often we undervalue or take for granted those skills and strengths that come naturally to us. What problems do you really enjoy solving or what problems do you feel passionate about trying to solve. This awareness will allow you to focus on what you're innately good at doing. When you decide to stand for something, you will then live in alignment with it. This will inspire you to come alive and flourish because the world needs your talent. This fulfillment brings you closer to discovering your why, which provides the motivation you will need to keep going.

Your why gives you meaning and direction. It provides you with clarity, helps you make decisions, and gives significance to life. The most classic childhood questions is simply "why?" Even from a young age, we know intuitively that the motive behind an action is the most important piece of any story. Likewise, knowing your "why" is a critical piece to living with intention. It answers why you want something. This is just like asking, why is this important? The key here is that the more important something is to us, the more likely we will continue doing it. For example, we seek good schools for our children because we want them to be successful or even safe. With success or safety as motivating factors, some parents will drive their children all the way across town with the hopes of achieving that end. Similarly, your why supports your purpose, fueling you to try again and work harder. The more significant your why, the more likely you will remain committed to something. You get a laser-beam focus because your why is that important. Think for a moment about a laser. It is basically focused energy. The basic idea of a laser is simple. It's a tube that concentrates light over and over again until it emerges as a really powerful beam. It is powerful enough to cut through steel and even zoom miles into the sky. Likewise, a clear sense of purpose enables you to focus your efforts on what matters most. It compels you to find a way or make one regardless of the odds or obstacles[7].

Once your why is clearly identified, your how will just show up. You won't even know where it came from. We have all heard stories of people finding strength they didn't even know they had when faced with a crisis, including moving cars, breaking down doors or lifting three times their weight. Your how works similarly to a crisis situation because it you will have to use courage, energy and determination that you didn't know you had.

Howard Thurmon, civil rights leader, once wrote, "Don't ask yourself what the world needs; ask yourself what makes you come alive, then go do that. Because what the world needs is people who have come alive." Think about what inspires you to come alive and flourish. The word inspire comes from the Latin, meaning "to breathe life into." When you are working on a life goal, your why, you feel more alive because that inspiration that you have is fueling you with the oxygen needed to breathe. That thing that inspires you is much bigger than being rich or acquiring fame. It is about tapping into what you are passionate about. Your passion leads you to your purpose. When you can focus all of your attention on that, you become a force.

Journey to Amazing

Creating a "why statement" becomes part of your personal brand. Your "why statement" will help people understand why you do what you do. First, start by asking yourself the *who* and *what* statements: *Who am I?* This could be, for example, a dancer, mother, builder, etc. *What do I want out of life?* This could range from peace to a palace. Next, ask your why statement: *Why do I want this?* This is just like asking, why is this important? The key here is that the more important something is to us, the more likely we are to continue doing it. Think of your why statement like a mission statement. Take time to write your own statement. You want a statement that gives you a sense of purpose and drives you day-in and day-out. Here is an example:

My mission is to act as an agent of change in my family, my friends and my community. I will utilize all of my God-given talents and will operate with passion, purpose and power in all aspects of my life. I will be led by love and not controlled by fear. Through this focus, I will give more than I take and remain humble and grateful. I will build generational wealth and be a positive role model for my daughter.

11.

TAKING THE NEXT STEP

You say, "I know what I want to do (or am called to do), but how do I get there?" That question can be as intimidating as uncovering one's purpose. For some, the mission may seem too daunting or, in fact, impossible. Marshawn Evans Daniels, the 2002 Miss America runner-up, who is now an accomplished author and speaker, said, "The size of your next step is not as important as the direction."

We don't always have to have all the details. The most important thing is to be willing to take a step. Do *something* toward fulfilling your calling. It can be as simple as making a phone call to ask for professional guidance. The universe is waiting for you to take a step, and then it will yield the other steps. Maybe not all at once, but eventually, you will see a clear path if you just move toward it and keep going. This all requires faith to take the first step and faith to believe the rest will unfold as you move forward.

Dreams are just an idea until you take the first step, but we tend to procrastinate when it comes to taking that first step. Why is taking that first step so difficult? Perfectionism is a major hindrance. We tend to want to make things perfect. You should not wait until the situation is perfect because the situation will never be perfect. Perfection is not practical, and in most cases, we use it as an excuse for procrastination. In life, people make errors, so that's why pencils have erasers. This is why computer keyboards have delete and backspace keys. Similarly, seeking the approval of others also hinders us from stepping out on faith. There will always be opposition, and that is typical. If we wait until there is a consensus, we will never start. We also often let our lack of mastery hamper us from taking that initial step. While you need to have a good skill set, you don't need to have it mastered before starting. In fact, you will learn much more by doing than by waiting to learn. Doing allows you to hone your skill much faster than just learning a theory. Finally, one of the greatest impediments to taking the next step is failing to identify or recognize our immediate resources. Somehow, many people feel they lack what they need to achieve their dreams, while overlooking the resources they already have. If you don't have arms, use your legs. If you don't have butter, use oil. If you aren't that smart, call on people in your life who are. The proverb "Necessity is the mother of invention" says it all. Find a way with what you have. Eventually, you will attract all that you need.

We all have dreams. Some dream of lavish lifestyles while others dream of world peace. The dreams that I am referring to are neither daydreams nor the ones that you have when your eyes are closed. They are also more than just wishful thinking. I am referring to dreams as highly desirable goals that we fully intend to realize. The only true way to make dreams become reality is that

> *"Go confidently in the direction of your dreams. Live the life you have imagined."*
>
> – Henry David Thoreau

you must move toward them purposefully and consistently. It all starts with a decision, and making a good one is crucial to your happiness. All of us are confronted with various decisions daily. Some have minimal consequences and represent a simple choice, while others are potentially life-changing, causing us much contemplation.

Those who are successful have not been lucky, but rather they have made a series of good decisions. There is an art to making good decisions. It *always* begins with honesty. It is almost impossible or highly unlikely to make a good decision in the absence of truth. Lying to yourself, believing someone else's lie, ignoring the facts or simply deciding to go against your better judgment, will most certainly yield a negative outcome. Similarly, people who tend to make hasty decisions that are driven by fear or selfishness, most often choose wrong.

Because the actualization of your dreams is dependent upon what decisions you make, careful consideration should be taken. Many people and companies use decision-making models to help them come up with the best possible outcome. The "rational decision-making" approach is a traditional model that consists of structured sequential steps. Usually these steps progress from problem/opportunity identification to the selection of preferred alternatives. Many of us use the "intuition decision-making" approach, which is less structured and places more emphasis on feelings, perceptions and judgments.

Either way, there are general phases to making good decisions. The first thing is always to identify the actual decision to be made by challenging the outcome you want to achieve. For instance, you may want to earn more money, so you believe the decision is whether you should start your own business or not. This, however, is not the *actual* decision. Your focus should instead be on whether earning more money will actually solve your issue. Maybe you need to lower your expenses, which can have the same net effect. Then determine if entrepreneurship is the best route to earning more money. Notice that lots of other questions came before whether you should start a business. The principle here is that you should always question the virtue of your desired outcome first because if you have the wrong goal, you will definitely make the wrong decision. If, for example, you say you want to have a big wedding, so you try to decide details like the size of the wedding party, venue and so forth. But again, you should first attack the notion of wanting a big wedding. Can I afford it? Why do I want a big wedding?

Usually the toughest part is actually deciding what to do. Once you gather facts and brainstorm about the choices, this will allow you to make an informed decision. Though, there will be many options, always choose the one that is most compatible with your values, interests and abilities. When you make a decision, stand boldly in it while monitoring your progress. Always be willing to change course or pause if feedback shows you that elements of your decision need to be altered. This requires humility.

We all begin with a distance between where we are and where we want to be. The goal is to narrow the distance until it no longer exists. As we draw our dreams closer to us while moving simultaneously towards them, this closes the gap.

Journey to Amazing

Before we can do anything else, you need to clearly define exactly what your dreams are. You should be very precise. This is not the time to be general; the universe doesn't answer half-hearted pleas. You need to be very specific. You are coupling the Law of Attraction and action in order to manifest your dreams. The Law of Attraction refers to the philosophy that "like attracts like." Thus, by focusing on positive thoughts, a person brings positive experiences into his or her life, and the inverse is true for negative thoughts. This is why we must focus on what we do want rather than what we don't want.

One of the best ways for you to get really clear is to write down a detailed description of exactly what you want to accomplish, your goal. Then write down the next logical step and each step after that.

Goal: _____

Step 1: _____

Step 2: _____

Step 3: _____

Some people attempt to attract their goals without taking much action. Others choose to act on their goals without the added advantage of also clearly defining their objectives. Action alone can bring positive results, but it is much faster to combine the two techniques. One of the reasons that setting goals is so important to the Law of Attraction is that goal-setting aligns your energy with your desires, giving you needed focus.

UNIT 4
BEING THANKFUL

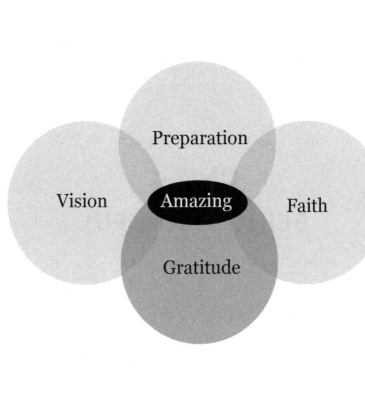

Gratitude is much more than simply saying "thank you." Its amazing power has the ability to shift us from focusing on the negative to focusing on what's positive in our lives. When we focus on the positive, we can see opportunities and resources that negative people are unable to even recognize. This is an ability we need in turning our passions into purpose, for amazing people are grateful people.

Practicing gratitude gives us a deeper connection to ourselves, the world around us and our Creator. Everything in our lives has the ability to improve when we are grateful. Research[8] has shown that gratitude can increase your mood, decrease your stress and drastically improve your overall levels of health and well-being. People who are grateful have higher incomes and are more satisfied personally and professionally. When we adopt gratitude as a lifestyle, we change our lives and world for the better, affecting the lives of those around us.

Think of gratitude as an emotional muscle that can and should be strengthened. Like any muscle you have, it needs to be exercised in order to be strengthened. Just a few minutes of gratitude a day can improve your life. We know that gratitude has physical, psychological and social benefits. It is not happy people who are thankful; it is thankful people who are happy.

Sometimes being grateful is easier said than done. For instance, you seek an opportunity and try to remain hopeful, but your close friends remind you of the impossible odds. How can you remain grateful for just having an opportunity when most everyone around you is doubtful? How can you have an attitude of gratitude when you've just had a terrible break-up or job loss? The answer is to always "hunt the good" in every situation, no matter how bad it appears. For example, losing your job can cause fear and anxiety, but perhaps, it was time to change your life's direction and look for a new career that is more suited to your passion and purpose.

In hunting the good, we don't have to act like negative situations don't occur, because "life happens" to each of us. It's healthy, in fact, to talk about our challenges, but when talking about a problem turns into complaining, that's precisely when we have to hunt the good. Complaining can become a habit, and this creates negativity that attracts even more negativity. Sometimes when life gets really difficult, we should remind ourselves of all the things we ought to be thankful for in general.

We are often so consumed with our daily routines and obligations that we may take family and even the people closest to us for granted. Showing gratitude for even small things, like having a family and friends, can cause a significant mood change. We can find things to be thankful for everywhere, such as someone holding the door open, a friend who always provides encouragement, a bus driver who waits for you or your child, a janitor who helps you take things to your car, a waiter who gives you an extra drink, and a co-worker who is constantly lending a hand. We must recognize that blessings exist everywhere. Gratitude can turn a test into a testimony, transform common days into unforgettable experiences, turn routine jobs into joy, and change ordinary opportunities into extraordinary breaks.

12.

TREASURING THE CHALLENGE

Don't forget it's a privilege to fight this battle. You may be without a job, have an illness or facing a difficult situation of some kind, but there is always someone worse off than you. When going through difficult times, it's harder to see the good that exists amidst our troubles. The practice of gratitude can help us during our low points in life, turning our thoughts of despair into thoughts of goodness. We can view our worst situations with a grateful eye and know that being grateful makes us stronger, more resilient, healthier, and happier. Being more grateful for what we have can increase our happiness by 25 percent, according to University of California Psychology Professor Dr. Robert Emmons[9]. His research on gratitude's effects discovered that a person who expresses gratitude is able to cope more effectively with everyday stress, may show increased resilience in the face of trauma-induced stress, and may recover more quickly from illness while benefitting from greater physical health. He concluded that gratitude is one of the few things that can change people's lives in a measurable way.

When we "hunt the good" or train our minds to the find the good in every situation, life truly becomes happier. The quality of your thoughts affects the quality of your life. It puts you on a different frequency. This doesn't mean that you accept the unfavorable situation in your life; it simply means that your focus is on the many things that are going right rather than wrong. For some, this is difficult, but if you continuously practice having gratitude, it becomes a way of life. The result: everything in our lives has the opportunity to improve along with our outlook.

The simplest form of thankfulness is for being alive, having the opportunity to experience creation. The only appropriate response to this gift is gratefulness. Before the day begins is an excellent time to reflect on all there is to be grateful for in life, remembering that it could always be worse. This starts the day with feelings of hope, peace and happiness. As soon as you wake up, you can say, "Thank you for this day." This starts our day on a good note instead of starting off with negative thoughts and worry.

> *"Yesterday's the past, tomorrow's the future, but today is a gift. That's why it's called the present."*
>
> - Bill Keane

I once heard about an experiment a school teacher did with the children in her class. They made three groups of plants that they watered exactly the same, but the only difference was how the students interacted with the plants. The first group lavished the plants with attention and said nice things to them. The second group did nothing but make negative comments about the plants. The third group ignored the plants as much as possible. As you might expect, the first group's plants thrived, and the second were small and stunted. The third group was even worse than the second group, appearing small, weak and dying. In a 1986 interview, England's Prince Charles discussed his gardening habits, saying, "I just come and talk to the plants, really. Very important to talk to them; they respond."[10] We may not realize it, but this is the way some of us live. We take pieces of it for granted by ignoring. We wake up in the morning and open two gifts: our eyes. We don't give a second thought that throughout the night our hearts kept beating, our lungs were filled with air, and blood was running throughout our body without us having to do a thing.

I grew up in a very traditional Southern Baptist church. During the devotional part of the service, the deacons would pray, "Thank you God for letting me wake up in my right mind!" As a young girl, I didn't have a clue what that meant. I would think, *well, who else's mind would they wake up with?* As I got older, especially when I started in my career, I understood it better. It's a blessing to have a sound mind. Small things like this we take for granted. We ignore so much of the goodness in our lives, only missing it when it is gone. Gratitude helps to consciously and intentionally have more appreciation, which leads to positive thinking. This attitude of gratitude guards us from taking life for granted.

We are sadly mistaken when we express a sense of entitlement, as if the world owes us something when it is we who owe the world. Service is the rent that we pay for our life here on earth. Gratitude is the opposite of taking things for granted. When we express gratitude, it makes what we have enough rather than eternally searching. Ironically, by being thankful for what we do have, we open our space for it to become more. When you transform your perspective about life, your life will change its perspective about you. No longer are you a victim or a complainer, disgruntled with life. You are an overcomer and thankful, treasuring life in its simplest form. Once you understand and accept that it is a privilege to be here, then you will honor this life. It will, in turn, honor you with more opportunities and new resources.

Journey to Amazing

Training your mind to see the good in every situation will be one of the best steps you can take in creating an empowering, abundant life. It's so much easier to give into negative thinking. If you challenge yourself to always find the positives, you will grow as a person, and your life will quickly give you more reasons to smile and enjoy the journey.

Journaling is a powerful tool. Successful weight-loss programs have participants keep food journals because it helps them be cognizant of what they are eating. I have clients keep journals for various reasons, including monitoring their dreams, externalizing their feelings, and especially listing what they are thankful for. Writing things down is a powerful way to focus your attention, keep track of life, create a permanent record for the future, and much more. The very act of writing things down helps to get them lodged into your long-term memory. As such, buy a small journal or notebook where, each day, you can write down something good about every situation. When you are really upset or stressed, just pull out your journal as a reminder that all is not lost.

You can also start a gratitude jar. Every week, write down things that happen in your life that you are thankful for. They can be small things like someone helping you with your bags or big things like landing a major contract. Write them all down and put them in the jar. The idea is to keep you constantly hunting for these treasures in your life. You cannot complain or maintain negative thoughts at the same time as having an attitude of gratitude. You are either thankful or not.

13.

GIVING WITHOUT RESERVATION

It doesn't matter if you're the giver or the receiver, giving evokes gratitude. It instills gratitude in the recipient and triggers an expression of gratitude in the giver, who is thankful that he or she was able to do it. When we give, we not only help the immediate recipient of our gift, but we also create a ripple effect of generosity through our community. A study by James Fowler of the University of California, San Diego, and Nicholas Christakis of Harvard showed that when one person behaves generously, it inspires observers to behave generously as well toward different people. Their research[11] found that philanthropy could spread by three degrees: from person to person to person to person. The researchers stated, "Each person in a network can influence dozens

> *"We make a living by what we get, but we make a life by what we give."*
>
> - Winston Churchill

or even hundreds of people, some of whom he or she does not know and has not met."

There is a great feeling and satisfaction that comes with giving, but the best feeling is witnessing the gratitude of the beneficiary. This is one reason volunteerism is something important in my life. In one charitable organization that I've worked with, it requires the participants to volunteer and give back. Even without the requirement to volunteer, most participants want to help because it makes them feel good. It's no coincidence that giving elicits feel-good emotions. Giving has also been linked to the release of oxytocin, a hormone (also released during sex and breast feeding) that induces feelings of warmth, euphoria, and connection to others. All things work together in this universe, and we are no different. [12]

Giving is a key aspect to personal happiness. Charitable work can provide meaning and a sense of greater purpose. We tend to give to those things to which we are fervent. Those passions that are directly tied to our life's purpose make giving that much easier. You can't live a life of purpose without giving being a part of it. It is through giving that we enrich and perpetuate both our own lives and the lives of others. By helping others, we truly help ourselves. Giving back makes us feel that we have a purpose, a mission, a calling, and that our efforts matter to others. Enriching the lives of others makes us all wealthier. True wealth is not acquired through worldly possessions, but by leading a fulfilling life. It helps us build stronger social connections. As social animals, we survive as a species when we cooperate with others and care for those in need. Thus, from an evolutionary and socio-biological perspective, we are wired to help others within our community, and doing so helps all of us survive and thrive.

In his book "The Hidden Splendor," spiritual teacher Shree Rajneesh, also known as Osho, wrote:

Gautam Buddha used to say to his disciples, "After meditating, when you are feeling full of joy, peace, and silence, share your silence, your peace, your blissfulness with the whole of existence—with men, with women, with trees, with animals, with birds—with all that exists, share it. It is not a question whether someone deserves it or not. The more you share it, the more you will get it." He added, "The farther your blessings reach, the more and more blessings will shower on you from all directions. Existence always gives you back more than you have given to it."

One man who was a great admirer of Gautam Buddha raised his hand and said, "I can share my blessings, my joy, with the whole of existence. Please just allow me one exception: I cannot share with my neighbor. I am ready to share with all the animals, all the birds, all the trees, except that one neighbor who is so nasty. You don't know about him; otherwise, you yourself would have said, 'You can have a few exceptions.'"

Buddha replied, "You don't understand what I am saying. If even your neighbor is not your neighbor, then how can birds, animals and trees be your friends and your neighbors? So practice just that one exception first; forget about the whole universe. You are already prepared to share your joy with everybody else; share your joy with your neighbor instead."[13]

There is no such thing as selective giving. When you give, you must give without stipulations or conditions. You must give without reservation. According to the late Indian philosopher Osho:

When people say, "We will give only to worthy people, to deserving people," these are excuses for not giving. Who is unworthy? If existence accepts a person, and the sun does not deny him light, and the trees does not deny him their shade, and the roses do not deny him their fragrance… if existence accepts him, who are you to think whether he is worthy or unworthy? His being alive is enough proof that existence accepts him as he is[14].

When I was younger, my father would give money to the men who always stood outside the neighborhood store. Depending on his mood, he would follow it with a joke or a word of wisdom. It was obvious to me that the beneficiaries were going to buy a bottle of alcohol. I would look at them in disgust and ask, "Why did you give him that money?"

My father explained that it is our job to give; it's not our job to determine what the receiver does with it. "God loves a cheerful giver," he would remind me. While I'm certain that the men outside the store didn't use the money to buy food, I came to understand that my only job was to give without reservations.

When you give with a pure heart and cheerful spirit, the universe recognizes it. "Conditional giving," said Osho, "is not giving at all. And those giving should not ask for gratitude in response. On the contrary, the giver should feel grateful that his gift has not been refused. Then giving becomes a tremendous ecstasy. This is how your heart grows, how your consciousness expands, how your darkness disappears, how you become more and more light, more and more close to the divine[15]." Once you realize that by giving you don't lose but you get more, your whole life structure will go through a transformation. The more you give your love, your compassion, your energy, and your kindness, the more you will find that the generosity of the universe and blessings will flow in your life from all directions.

There are countless stories throughout history and various religious that reference giving. In the Bible, the apostle Paul wisely cautioned the Corinthians, "Remember this: Whoever sows sparingly will also reap sparingly, and whoever sows generously will also reap generously" (2 Corinthians 9:6). Indeed, "Good will come to him who is generous" (Psalm 112:5). So, having a benevolent spirit and being a cheerful giver is key to an abundant life of purpose.

Journey to Amazing

There are many ways to give back, but following your passions is key. You can easily donate items, volunteer at a soup kitchen or homeless shelter, be a scout leader, and the list could go on and on. When you give in your area of giftedness and where you passion lies, this makes the experience more fulfilling. If giving feels chore-like and task-oriented, then you're out of alignment with your purpose. Find something that you are passionate about, especially when you are working toward your purpose because this leads you directly to your purpose. Once you identify where you want to give your time, commit to it and stick with it. Watch the change you make in your own life, your community and the world as a whole.

14.

SHARING THE GIFT

Anything that makes you feel powerful, connected and aligned with your truth does the same when shared. It doesn't matter if you're writing a song, baking pies or planning a company outing. Nothing that really calls you is ever for you alone. It must be shared in order to gain its value.

In fact, there is no gift ever given that is meant for you to keep for yourself. In 1843, Ralph Waldo Emerson reasoned in an essay titled "Gifts" that the only meaningful gift is sharing oneself. He wrote:

> Rings and jewels are not gifts, but apologies for gifts. The only gift is a portion of thyself. Thou must bleed for me. Therefore, the poet brings his poem; the shepherd, his lamb; the farmer, corn; the miner, a stone; the painter, his picture; the girl, a handkerchief of her own sewing.[16]

Our gifts can be found in the most sacred places within us, a place where both love and creativity exist. Our gifts are never

> *"The purpose of life is to discover your gift. The work of life is to develop it. The meaning of life is to give your gift away."*
>
> – David Viscott

lost, merely hidden sometimes. They tend to emerge wherever we feel the most vulnerable, passionate and authentic. These are our core gifts. Our core gifts need to be nourished if they are to flourish. This means that before you run out into the world, ready to use your superpowers, or personal gifts, you must first grow and gain knowledge. Even the greatest superheroes had to understand and develop their craft before venturing to save the world. For instance, Clark Kent, better known as Superman, took more than a decade to develop his superpowers. Just because he had superstrength and superspeed didn't mean that he was ready to save Earth from the Kryptonians. His human adoptive parents raised him with high morals and values, which was important because with great power comes great responsibility. Likewise, without the right efforts, we create the wrong results.

Giving is natural. In fact, it is essential to life. Everything in nature gives. The rain gives water to the crops. The crops provide work for the farmers. The farmers provide food for us. You see how this works. Our core gift must be shared in a way that touches others. When we witness our gifts' impact on others, we can truly feel worthy. It costs nothing to give, but it could cost you everything if you don't. When we are open to sharing our gifts, this will inevitably guide us to what matters most, such as giving back to our community or advocating for the underserved. However, if we ignore the opportunity to share, it can be self-injurious or even worse, suicide to our soul's existence.

When I first began researching about gifts and purpose, I came across an article that changed my belief system. It literally shifted the way I thought about my own gifts, and I began to incorporate this in my psychotherapy work. The article conferred that people should learn how to cultivate the opposite quality of their gift. I thought, *Why would someone want to do that and how?*

In order to develop your gift's complementary characteristic, we must first identify our core gift and then distinguish the opposite of it. Think about it this way. If, for example, you were a visionary, you would need to cultivate practicality in order for your creation to come to life. The practical person needs to cultivate his dreamer-self in order to create beauty in his life. The generous person needs to cultivate her "no."

Ironically, the less we have cultivated the opposite quality of our gifts, the more we will be attracted to people who carry that opposite quality in extreme ways. For instance, a person who has a benevolent spirit but can't set limits, will be inclined to attract someone who is great at taking but not so great at giving back. The more we cultivate these complementary qualities within ourselves, the more we'll find ourselves attracted to people who appreciate our gifts and who won't take advantage of us. Our core gift will always remain dominant. The goal is not to replace it, but to give it balance, to have it be respected.

When we take the time to cultivate and share our gifts, something amazing happens. We give our gifts wings in the world. We give them an opportunity to take flight and be shared with others everywhere. We owe it to ourselves to find our gift, and we owe it to the world to share it. We all have gifts to share and the potential to make a difference based on the way we live. Our potential will be released simply by showing up as who we really are and not as who we think we should be. By hiding our true presence, presenting the person we think we need to be rather than who we are, we deny the world the beautiful life they could have known. When we begin to operate in our authentic presence, this will not only release the gifts we have to give, but it also opens us up to receiving the gifts we need from others.

We don't have to start by trying to take over the world. Start sharing your gifts with those closest to you, those who are right in front of your face. Our relationships with others offer opportunities to give and receive each other's gifts. In order for these relationships to be meaningful, they must be supported by unconditional love. This permits us to see beyond our differences and embrace the opportunities to learn from the people we encounter on our life's journey. In this day and time, our community needs us, having an obligation to share our gifts that will make our community a better place.

People who are truly grateful for the gift they have been given are more likely to share their gifts than those who take it for granted or simply don't care. When we are proud of something, we typically want to show it off. Think about when you were proud of earning a good grade, passing a test or getting something you always wanted. You probably shared the news with anyone who would listen. Similarly, when we take pride in our gift, we want to share it. Research shows that there are actually emotional benefits from sharing positivity with others[17].

In sharing our gifts, we must be careful, however, not to allow those with a negative outlook to discourage us from sharing. Whether the negativity ranges from envy to self-hatred, other people's opinion should never dictate your willingness to share your core gift or cause you to question its significance. This is why we must share without expecting reciprocity. We give simply because it was given to us. When you know and apply this principle, you will truly be free and able to experience life on another level, one where passion and purpose collide.

Journey to Amazing

Start by asking yourself questions such as: what contributions am I making to my loved ones? What impact am I having on the environment? What sort of legacy am I creating? What will it take to live my best life? These are all life-changing questions that only you can answer. You already have all the clues you need to find out just what your gift is to the world. Now go out and share it, and allow yourself to be the greatest gift to the world.

Even when something bad happens, believe in abundance and know that plenty of opportunities will come your way. You have to share your wealth of positivity with the world. The best way that I found to do this is to simply be nice to other people as much as possible. No matter what, compliment others in some fashion. When you begin to share positivity, it comes back to you.

END NOTES

[1] Burke, Julian. (2009, Sept. 16). *Success Secrets – The Importance of Having a Vision*. Retrieved from http://www.dreammanifesto.com/success-secrets-importance-vision.html

[2] Ibid.

[3] Helgoe, Courtney. (2010, Nov.) *5 Gut Instincts You Shouldn't Ignore*. Retrieved from https://experiencelife.com/article/5-gut-instincts-you-shouldnt-ignore/

[4] Davenport, Jacob. (2011, Sept. 25) *The Tortoise and the Hare*. Retrieved from http://brightestbulb.net/entertainment/tortoise_and_hare/

[5] Ybarra, T.R. (1926, Aug. 6). "Gertrude Ederle Swims the Channel". *The New York Times*.

[6] Bloom, Steve. (2010). *The 3 Types of Fear That Can Hold You Back*. Retrieved from http://dosomethingcool.net/3-types-fear-hold/

[7] Warrell, Margie. (2013, Oct. 30). "Do You Know Your 'Why?' 4 Questions to Find Your Purpose". *Forbes*.

[8] Seligman MEP, et al. (July–Aug. 2005). "Empirical Validation of Interventions." *American Psychologist*: Vol. 60, No. 1, pp. 410–21.

[9] Emmons, R. A., & McCullough, M. E. (2003). "Counting Blessings Versus Burdens: An experimental investigation of gratitude and subjective well-being in daily life". *Journal of Personality and Social Psychology*, 84(2), 377-389.

[10] Stevenson, Alexa. (2008) "Probing Question: Does talking to plants help them grow?" *Penn State News*. University of Pennsylvania.

[11] Fowler, James H. Fowler and Christakis, Nicholas A. (2010). Proceedings of the National Academy of Sciences, Vol. 107 No. 10.

[12] Marsh, Jason, Suttie, Jill. (2010, Dec., 13). *Ways Giving Is Good for You*. Retrieved from http://greatergood.berkeley.edu/article/item/5_ways_giving_is_good_for_you

[13] Osho. (1987, March). *The Hidden Splendor: Discovering Your Inner Beauty*. English discourse series. Retrieved from https://www.oshorajneesh.com/download/osho-books/responses_to_questions/The_Hidden_Splendor.pdf

[14] Ibid.

[15] Ibid.

[16] Emerson, Ralph Waldo. (1843). *Gifts*. The Dial, Volume IV, Number

I, Page 93, Column 1. James Munroe and Company, Boston, Massachusetts.

[17] Lambert, N., Gwinn, A., Baumeister, R., Strachman, A., Washburn, I., Gable, S., and Fincham, F. (2012). *A Boost of Positive Affect: The Perks of Sharing Positive Experiences. Journal of Social and Personal Relationships* DOI: http://dx.doi.org/10.1177/0265407512449400

CPSIA information can be obtained
at www.ICGtesting.com
Printed in the USA
LVOW13s1240121217
559482LV00001B/1/P

9 780998 669410